Capability Brown in Kent

C000225952

Kent Gardens Trust

First published in 2016 by Kent Gardens Trust
Knowle Hill Farm, Ulcombe, Kent, ME17 1ES
www.kentgardenstrust.org.uk

ISBN 978-0-9934044-0-5

A CIP catalogue record for this book is available from the British Library

Designed and Typeset by Pamela Cuerden

Printed in Great Britain by

windsor
EST·1982
2 Sovereign Way, Tonbridge
01732 361558
info@windsor.uk.com
www.windsor.uk.com

*Cover image: Brown's Five Arch Bridge at North Cray Place
Courtesy of Lee Ricketts,
taken from youtu.be/rGMJd3ml37Y*

Capability Brown in Kent

Kent Gardens Trust

Location map

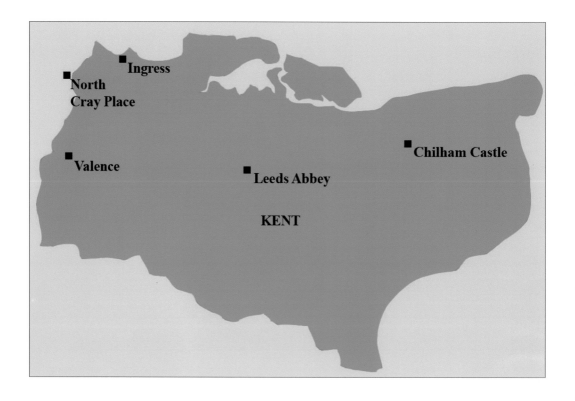

Ingress

North
Cray Place

Chilham Castle

Valence

Leeds Abbey

KENT

Contents

Preface

Lancelot 'Capability' Brown was involved with the design of only five sites in Kent and one of those, Chilham Castle, he changed only slightly. While the park and gardens at Chilham have survived more or less intact, the other four sites have not been treated kindly by the social and environmental changes which have taken place in the 250 years since he worked in Kent.

The proximity to London of places like North Cray Place and Ingress which, in the 18th century, attracted politicians and businessmen to use them as rural retreats, was also the cause of their decline in the 19th and 20th centuries as they became surrounded by commuter suburbs. It seems almost miraculous that anything at all of Brown's landscapes should have survived the urbanization of the outskirts of the city and, in the case of Ingress, appropriation by the merchant navy and industrial development.

Rather different influences have caused the decay of Brown's landscapes at Valence and Leeds Abbey but they have been no less devastating. Family disputes and long minorities have not infrequently led to the decline of great estates but, even so, it is extraordinary that the house and grounds of Leeds Abbey should have been abandoned within a generation of so much attention having been lavished upon it. The decline of Valence follows a more familiar course of financial overstretch and declining family fortunes leading to the break-up of the estate into several separate ownerships.

When Kent Gardens Trust began to consider how to celebrate the tercentenary of Brown's birth in 1716, we might have been deterred from embarking on a review of the few sad remnants of his work in Kent. Even Chilham Castle which remains the fine landscape much as Brown saw it in 1777 is not a typical example of the great man's work as the changes he made there to the existing landscape were slight. But having decided that we wanted to mark the anniversary in a particularly Kentish way, we decided to explore the sites and publish the results; and so we commenced our research.

What we have unearthed has easily repaid the many hours spent in libraries and archives and in tracing the lost landscapes through bramble thickets and along hard pavements. We think that we have added a little to the sum of knowledge about this extraordinary genius whose work is so embedded in our concept of the English countryside that his landscapes appear to be entirely natural. We hope that this book will make people more alive to the history of the places where Brown worked and become aware of what remains of his designs. Is it too much to hope that they may be encouraged to place a higher value on the remaining elements of Brown's work and take steps to conserve them for future generations?

Although it has in some ways been dispiriting to find so little of Brown's landscapes still in existence in Kent, there have been some grounds for optimism and excitement. To find the lake and water works sleeping under a cloak of brambles at Leeds Abbey has been an extraordinary experience and we are hopeful that by making its owners aware of its history its future survival will be assured. At Ingress we uncovered a seeming collaboration between Brown and Sir William Chambers, his bitter enemy, leading to speculation about how they dealt with the situation without the benefits of modern counselling. A few vestiges of the landscape can still be seen within the surrounding streets. Reading contemporary letters from the owner of Chilham Castle recording Brown's advice and opinions has brought him to life in a remarkable way. Brown's landscape at North Cray Place, depicted on the front cover, no longer the private pleasure ground of a wealthy family, now gives pleasure to hundreds of local people to whom Brown's name and reputation may be completely unknown. Even at Valence, now a school, a golf course and private housing, Brown's lake still exists and perhaps sometime further restoration of other water features will delight schoolchildren in the future and awaken their latent aesthetic sensibilities to the benefit of future generations.

The only one of these sites which is open to the public is North Cray Place which is part of Foots Cray Meadows, ninety-seven hectares of parkland and woodland in the London Borough of Bexley. Chilham Castle is open regularly in the summer (the times can be found on its website at www.chilham-castle.co.uk) and under the National Gardens Scheme. Leeds Abbey, North Cray Place and Valence may be visited electronically via the research pages of our website at www.kentgardenstrust. org.uk. The park and gardens at Chilham Castle are included on the Historic England Register of special historic interest in England and the register entry can be found on its website at www.historicengland.org.uk

We hope that this book will interest garden historians and will also appeal to a wider readership including all those who value our landscape, and are interested in its history and in the work of one of our greatest and most influential designers of landscape.

Elizabeth Cairns, Chairman, Kent Gardens Trust

Acknowledgements

Kent Gardens Trust would like to thank all those who have taken part in this project and have given their time and expertise so generously. The chapters have been written by members of the KGT volunteer research group and reviewed by their peers. Virginia Hinze has kindly edited the text for which we are very grateful.

A surprising number of images and original documents have been discovered during the research process and we would like to thank the following organisations for their help, their support and for their kind permission to publish images: the British Library, the National Archives, Sir John Soane Museum, Kent History and Library Centre, Bexley Local Studies and Archive Centre, Kent Archaeological Society, London Metropolitan Archives, Kent Historic Environment Record and Bridgeman Images. Grateful thanks are also due to those who kindly gave permission to publish images from their private collections: John Lochen, Jacs Taylor-Smith, and Stuart and Tessa Wheeler. Thanks also to Rowan Blaik for his assistance to Liz Logan in the process of digital map-making from OS OpenData sources, to Anne Evans for the use of her research notes on earlier work at Ingress, and to Lee Ricketts who supplied the images of the Five Arch Bridge at North Cray Place.

It would not have been possible to publish this book without the very generous grants from the John Swire 1989 Charitable Trust, the Roger de Haan Charitable Trust, the Stanley Smith (UK) Horticultural Trust, the Rochester Bridge Trust, the Historic Houses Association and the Kent Archaeological Trust.

Kent Gardens Trust is also indebted to Richard Stileman for his invaluable support and advice on publishing and marketing the book, and to Pamela Cuerden whose unstinting efforts with page design and page make-up have enabled us to publish successfully.

Kent Gardens Trust:
Working for Kent's Garden Heritage

Kent Gardens Trust was established as a charitable trust in 1988 at a time when there was a growing recognition that gardens are under threat from development, changing lifestyles, neglect or ignorance; and that useful work could be done to raise public awareness of their importance, both as living historical records of social and aesthetic changes and also as valuable green spaces in a world dominated by roads, buildings, noise and pollution.

Over the last eight years, the Trust, with the support of Kent County Council, has been commissioned by the local authorities in Tunbridge Wells, Sevenoaks and Medway to update their records of parks and gardens and we are now working on sites in Dover District. The reports, based on rigorous historical research, provide vital information for planners and help to promote interest in and understanding of the history of parks and gardens in the county. They can be seen in the research section of the Kent Gardens Trust website at www.kentgardenstrust.org.uk and have been used for entries on the Parks and Gardens UK database at www.parksandgardens.org

The Trust has also undertaken individual commissions to research and record sites of historic importance which have been used to obtain restoration funding from the Heritage Lottery Fund, and to inform plans to restore both private and publicly owned parks and gardens.

As part of its mission to promote understanding in the history of gardens the Trust, again supported by Kent County Council, has produced a book on historic gardens in Kent: *Garden of England* by Elisabeth Hall and a survey of public parks in the county: *A Presentation of Parks.* We hope that this short book on Capability Brown's work in Kent, which contains much original research, will be thought a worthy continuation of this tradition.

The Trust has a programme of lectures on a range of interesting topics relating to garden history and design, and visits for our members to notable gardens. An annual newsletter contains articles on garden history and related subjects, news items and book reviews. The research group provides training and study days for volunteers who are involved in the research projects.

The Trust welcomes new members who are interested in joining the research group or who would enjoy the talks and visits with like-minded people. For more information on how to join and to read the reports of our research please visit: www.kentgardenstrust.org.uk

Foreword

As a devoted admirer, I welcome the first in-depth publication to chart 'Capability' Brown's five works within the 'Garden of England'.

Let us applaud Kent Gardens Trust researchers who have pieced together remnant evidence to re-evaluate his major contribution to the liberating design story of the English landscape garden in Kent. Three hundred years since Brown was born into a Northumberland farming community, their painstaking surveys and interpretation of accounts throw new light on integrated improvements. His great earthworks, roads and reservoirs changed the way landowners appreciated and ran their estates. Here was a remarkable polymath celebrity who rose to be George III's Master Gardener.

By the time of his first foray into the county, Brown headed a successful, professional, wide-ranging architectural and engineering practice, offering horticultural, forestry and drainage advice in both flood and drought. Rivals mocked his fruit-growing expertise in state-of-the-art walled gardens, such as at Ingress, and coveted his dynamic leadership and loyal foremen. Hops played a part. Clients were advised to build nurseries as well as brew-houses to implement ambitious planting plans and keep the workforce happy and healthy. Thomas Heron's letters at Chilham Castle bear witness to the stimulation and morale boost Brown's arrival caused.

His links with Kent are more than meets the eye, none more politically intriguing than with a War Office paymaster and agent to the regiments. John Calcraft MP was so enthused by Brown's 'zeal and projects' at Ingress, as also at Luton for Lord Bute, that he commissioned him to develop similar potential at Leeds Abbey.

Amazing pictorial, cartographic and financial evidence, as revealed here, is compared with other surviving Brown works elsewhere in the country. This will stimulate the reader's imagination regarding the 'lost' landscapes. Who can forget the magnificent Hill Park cascade in JP Neale's illustration? We learn of house alterations here and a growing dependence on Henry Holland Jr, soon to become both son-in-law and partner, though building a church was uppermost in the Earl of Hillsborough's plans. Whether a client's faith, or an expression of his own Christian philosophy, Brown drew minds to the ultimate Creator, here with a memorable vista to Canterbury Cathedral and there to a converted chapel on a hillside set off by cherry trees. We picture an impressive approach through dappled North Cray woods and contrasting open parkland pasture. We sense the gentle rise of his sturdy five-arch bridge spanning his mirror-lake which prompted visitors to take in entrancing views of the house and St James' Church.

There will always be more questions than answers to the Brown narrative - perhaps thankfully. He knew that, by careful levelling, perfectionist planting and hidden engineering 'to keep all in view very neat', every good garden could develop a frisson of mystery. His bookplate motto, now on display at his final resting-place, St Peter and Paul Church, Fenstanton, Cambridgeshire, was Nunquam minus solus quam cum solus, 'Never less alone than when alone'.

Horace Walpole was probably the first to promote in writing the amusing nickname 'Capability', which underplayed his inventive genius interwoven with spatial awareness and artistic eye for line, colour and texture. J.M.W. Turner began to paint Brown landscapes in all their 'infinite variety' from the age of twelve. Meanwhile, equally motivated to tour England's great gardens, Hermann von Pückler Muskau (1785-1871) returned to create a landscape park in his homeland. This German prince repeatedly acclaimed Capability Brown in his journal, more appropriately, as the 'Shakespeare of Garden Arts'.

Kent Gardens Trust's well-timed tercentenary tribute signals the need for a wider awareness of the holistic management of landscape, underpinned by forward-thinking water-engineering, perhaps Capability Brown's greatest legacy. As William Gilpin acknowledged, water continues to be 'as much use as blood in a body'. Enjoy this deeply-probing book. It informs local understanding of Kent's topography and, long after his last tree has fallen, will facilitate restorations and new settings to keep some theatre and 'Brownian' sense of place alive in this delightful garden county.

Steffie Shields, January 13, 2016

Introduction

The year 2016 marks the tercentenary of the birth of Lancelot 'Capability' Brown (1716-1783) (fig.1), the foremost exponent of the 18th-century English Landscape Movement. From modest beginnings as an apprentice gardener in his home county of Northumberland, he rose to become one of England's leading landscape architects with over 200 commissions firmly attributed to his name.[1] Five of these commissions, the subject of this book, were in Kent, which Brown executed between the late 1760s and the early 1780s, during the most prolific and lucrative years of his career.

At the start of his career, in the early 1730s, Brown would have been aware of the marked, though gradual, transition from the controlled formality of 17th-century garden designs, with their long avenues of clipped trees, topiary and elaborate parterres, towards freer, more naturalistic styles. Until the early 18th century, most of England's prestigious country estates and royal palaces reflected Dutch and French influences, in particular, the school of André Le Nôtre (1613-1700). The move away from French formalism, symbolising King Louis IV's absolute power in France, coincided with a change in political attitudes in England. There was a marked shift away from autocratic rule towards a more liberal constitution, heralded by the Glorious Revolution of 1688 and confirmed by the subsequent rise of the Whigs. It also marked the age of Enlightenment which witnessed advances in society through various fields including philosophical thought, poetry and literature. To practitioners of the new English Landscape School, the ideas of the landscape gardener Charles Bridgeman (1690-1738) and the poetry of Alexander Pope (1688-1744) became increasingly relevant, as landscape architects were encouraged to consider the 'genius of the place' in its natural surroundings.

Similar preoccupations were also felt in polite society, many of whom travelled to Europe on the Grand Tour to broaden their cultural horizons, particularly in the fields of art and architecture. For some, the Grand Tour offered an opportunity to formulate ideas for a new garden style in England, often inspired by the pastoral idylls of the Roman Campagna, and captured on canvas by artists such as Nicholas Poussin (1594-

Figure 1.
Portrait of Lancelot
'Capability' Brown,
c.1770-75, by Richard
Cosway (1742-1821)©
*Courtesy: Private
Collection/Bridgeman
Images*

1665), Claude Gellée, known as Le Lorrain (1604/5-1682), and
Gaspard Dughet (1615-1675). During the early 18th century,
images of these idealised landscapes were brought to a wider
public as prints, and copies of similar scenes proliferated
throughout Europe. It was also at this time, between 1715
and 1725, that the publication of Colen Campbell's *Vitruvius
Britannicus* heralded the demise of the Baroque era by fostering
Renaissance principles in architecture: the Baroque was
equated with 'excess' and 'artificiality', whereas Renaissance
architecture was regarded as 'pure' and therefore more

13

'natural'. The *Britannicus* also coincided with Leoni's edition of Andrea Palladio's (1508-1580) seminal work, *I Quattro Libri dell' Architettura*, published and translated by Nicholas Dubois in 1715.

One of the earliest exponents of more naturalistic garden styles, and Renaissance principles in architecture, was the former painter turned architect, William Kent (1685-1748). His architectural studies in Italy between 1709 and 1719 coincided with those of Robert Boyle, the 3rd Earl of Burlington (1694-1753), the foremost advocate for Palladianism. Working in collaboration with the Earl, Kent would create his own vision of Arcadia at Chiswick. Indeed, Chiswick heralded the birth of Palladianism in England with the building of the villa, an interpretation of Palladio's Villa Rotonda (1550-51) in Vicenza. Much of Palladio's 16th-century architecture 'evoked the era of the Roman Republic when Rome was revered as a model for constitutional government and freedom'.[2] The analogy with the Villa Rotonda was, therefore, an important one for those who championed British liberty and constitutional reform. In the gardens of Chiswick (which Burlington opened to the general public), Kent placed greater emphasis on more natural forms

Figure 2. The Palladian Bridge at Stowe
Courtesy: Peter Dean

by creating gently sloping lawns down to the meandering river, but this was tempered by splayed, formal avenues of clipped hedging (a patte d'oie) with contrived views and vistas offering unexpected glimpses of classical garden statuary, a bagnio and a domed pavilion.

Kent adopted similar principles at Stowe when invited 'to soften' Charles Bridgeman's formalism previously created for Richard Temple, the 1st Viscount Cobham (1675-1749). And it was at Stowe, in 1741, that Brown was appointed master gardener, having first honed his skills in planting, earth moving and dam building at Sir William Loraine's Northumbrian Kirkharle Hall estate. At Stowe, he would also turn his attention to architecture and oversee the alterations to a Palladian Bridge (fig.2) and the execution of a Gothic temple. Over the next ten years, whilst still at Stowe, Brown began to forge his own identity and aesthetic as a landscape architect, securing commissions including those at Newnham Paddox in Warwickshire, Croome Park in Worcestershire and Petworth in Sussex (the latter quintessentially early Brown) to name but a few (fig.3).

It has long been recognised that, when Brown was given a free rein, his natural inclination was to sweep away formal gardens, particularly from the principal building, and replace them with a sea of turf which often sloped down to newly-created serpentine lakes. Inspired by Bridgeman's designs,[3] he would often create a ha-ha (or fosse as Brown would call it) to blur the boundary between the main house and the parkland beyond; he planted evergreens and single specimens of cedar of Lebanon close to the house; but he also favoured indigenous trees such as ash, oak, elm, lime and beech to create curved perimeter belts, scatter them as specimen trees or more usually plant them in clumps. He would also contrive views and vistas along meandering pathways and carriage drives around the parkland. It has also long been recognised that Brown was an architect, albeit with no formal training who, with the support of others, became responsible for the building of many houses, garden buildings and bridges. But it is as a landscape gardener with a particular design aesthetic that was forged into a national identity for which he has become most celebrated.

Figure 3.
View of Petworth
towards the lake
Courtesy: T.P.
Holland under
Creative Commons

In Kent, there are five sites, all relatively small-scale, which have been attributed to Brown with certainty: Ingress, Leeds Abbey, Valence, Chilham, and North Cray Place (the last, following boundary changes, is now situated within the London Borough of Bexley). These sites comprise the subject of this book in the form of individual chapters. In an attempt to broaden our understanding of Brown's work, each chapter seeks to explore the extent to which his input reflected his overall design aesthetic as we understand it, and how his patrons and contemporaries helped to support and inform his ideas during a period of social, economic and political change.

Unsurprisingly, all five sites, though diverse in their topographical and geological nature, reveal elements of landscape design which typify Brown's work and exemplify his skills as a water engineer. He altered the contours of existing ponds and water courses, widened rivers, moved large banks of earth, built dams and weirs in order to create large serpentine lakes; he planted sinuous tree belts so as to obscure boundary lines, outbuildings and kitchen gardens that would otherwise offend 18th-century sensibilities; he planted specimen holm oaks to stand alone whilst other trees, deciduous and fir, were planted in clumps within the parkland and near to the principal building to form a backdrop; axial lime avenues were removed and replaced with circuitous carriage drives, whilst woods were thinned to create views and vistas along the way.

The Kent sites also show that Brown, rather than starting from scratch, often developed landscape work already undertaken by others in a naturalistic style. Brown took the English Landscape Movement to new heights but clearly he did not invent it. At Valence, a designed landscape with a serpentine river existed long before Brown arrived; William Chambers (1723-1796) worked on the pleasure grounds at Ingress before Brown; and at Chilham a more naturalistic style, including the removal of an avenue of trees, was introduced in the mid-18th century before Brown's commission in the late 1770s. Some of the sites, however, illustrate aspects that are less typical of Brown's work. At Chilham, for example, it is particularly notable that the formal terracing, which is not usually associated with Brown's aesthetic, was left largely intact. Brown's association with kitchen gardens may also appear surprising, but plans for a greenhouse (Chilham), new greenhouses and hothouses (Ingress and Valence), and a complete kitchen garden (Ingress) have all been attributed to Brown. At Chilham, he submitted plans for a greenhouse although the kitchen garden was not moved. At Ingress, however, Brown not only moved the kitchen garden, but built a new one at some distance away from the house. Certainly by this time, in the late-18th century, greenhouses, orangeries and conservatories had become architectural features in their own right. The fashion for growing tender exotics such as melons, oranges and pineapples was becoming more common, but for wealthy landowners it was more about status and prestige than self-sufficiency. Brown would certainly have understood how important these developments were to his patrons. By 1764 he had been appointed Master Gardener to George III at the Hampton Court and Richmond palaces. He would therefore have been very familiar with the development of the Royal Botanic Gardens at Kew, undertaken for the Dowager Princess of Wales between 1757 and 1763 by Chambers and John Stuart, the 3rd Earl of Bute (1713-1792). Furthermore, Brown's ideas would have been particularly influenced by the 6th Earl of Coventry (1722-1809), for whom the growing of exotic fruits and rare plants at Croome Park became a lifelong obsession, so much so that Croome has been described as being 'inferior only to Kew'. Brown began working for Coventry in 1749 and continued to advise the Earl until the end of his life. Croome was reputedly Brown's 'favourite residence; he never found himself so much at home as when there, nor at any time so happy.'[4]

Brown's work on other aspects of architecture, perhaps not fully appreciated, is also illustrated in Kent. The fashion for diverse architectural styles in the 18th century would have been very familiar to Brown, particularly those constructed by Chambers at Kew, including a Moorish Alhambra and a mosque, and at Ingress, a Chinese pagoda and an Ionic temple. Yet Brown did not share Chambers' fervour in this respect. Brown's architectural style was generally far more restrained, and he is best known for designing buildings in either the Palladian or Gothic styles.

Brown's approval of classic Palladianism was certainly reinforced in the design of the mansion's facade and the model dairy at Valence. And his approval of Gothic architecture was also made evident at Valence as it was elsewhere outside Kent. At Valence, he is attributed with the building of the

Figure 4.
The church of St. Mary Magdalene at Croome, built by Brown in 1759

Gothic Temple for the Earl of Hillsborough's (1718-1793) garden: unfortunately, the temple does not survive, and no plans or images have come to light. Whether it echoed the Gothic Temple at Stowe with which Brown would have been very familiar during his early career, we shall probably never know. But it may well have been an influence, and Brown would design a number of other Gothic buildings (often with the collaboration of other architects) such as the Church of St. Mary Magdalene at Croome (fig.4), and the greenhouse at Burghley, the latter arguably to preserve the integrity of the Gothic elements of the house.

It is notable that Brown appeared keen to preserve the integrity of existing architecture as he did at Burghley, while less keen to preserve the formality of historic landscapes. This may be due to Brown placing far more faith in his natural ability as a landscape gardener than as an architect. It is certainly true that in this respect he looked to contemporaries for support throughout his career. Both Sir Robert Taylor (1714-1788) and Robert Adam (1728-1792) designed a number of Brown's interiors, and for the Kent commissions Brown relied upon his son-in-law, Henry Holland the younger (1745-1806), for the interior designs of the Valence mansion and Leeds Abbey. It is regrettable that evidence of their collaboration is fragmentary, nearly all of Holland's office papers having been destroyed following Holland's death. But the primary evidence that has been unearthed does provide valuable insights into the particular importance of their collaboration in Kent.

Although Brown had many supporters and collaborators, he was not without his critics even during his lifetime. Chambers was a severe critic and their relationship was particularly uneasy. Towards the end of the Ingress commission, Chambers' antagonism towards Brown had probably reached its height. Brown had won the commission for the rebuilding of the house at Claremont for Lord Clive of India, who had rejected Chambers' proposals in favour of Brown's. It is intriguing to imagine how they worked together at Ingress, particularly as the two commissions coincided. Nevertheless, any personal animosity Brown may have felt towards Chambers did not affect his overall vision for Ingress: he ensured that views of the house from the river were not obscured by trees, and his planting was designed to highlight Chambers' Palladian-style architecture.

Brown's commissions in Kent also illustrate some of the social and economic developments that underpinned the gradual shift to a more natural style of landscaping. Although enclosure of land began much earlier, by the 1770s it had become much easier for landowners to expand their property and remove public rights of way that fell within their boundaries. By then, local magistrates could approve major changes that previously required an act of Parliament. The estates at Valence, Ingress and Chilham became much larger in the 18th century and Brown actively encouraged the ambitions of major landowners as they diverted roads and moved buildings to create larger areas of both parkland and units of agricultural production. Rising economic prosperity in the second half of the 18th century bolstered the position of both the major landowners and the gentry, and also allowed a rising 'middle class' of professionals, such as lawyers and government officials, to become landowners. The owners of Chilham, Leeds Abbey, Ingress, and North Cray Place, all had professional roles even if these roles often brought them into close contact with the landed aristocracy.

Brown's influence also extended into political life. His commission at Leeds Abbey strongly suggests that he took it upon himself to manage some of the difficult and complicated political relationships that existed at the time. Late-18th century politics were dominated by factions. There were no political parties as such but rival groupings, mostly describing themselves as Whigs of one form or another. Given his charismatic nature, and his connections with those holding influential political offices, Brown was uniquely placed to help soothe some of these fierce rivalries. It was of course in his interests to do so as he wanted as many commissions as possible, and did not want to reject a business opportunity simply because of the political persuasions of the patron. So far, there has been little discussion by commentators about Brown's potential role as a political go-between, but it is clear that this was another of his many attributes.

In many ways, the five sites in Kent re-affirm our understanding of Brown's naturalistic approach to landscape design, and a particular aesthetic that he replicated up and down the country. Notwithstanding the challenging terrain in Kent, the 'genius of the place' with its pre-existing, centuries-old woodlands, deer parks, rivers and watercourses, certainly helped Brown to realise his vision. The sites illustrate Brown's role as an architect of both Palladian and Gothic-style buildings; and they also reinforce the notion that Brown could not ignore the rising tide of fashion, particularly his patrons' need to acquire sophisticated kitchen gardens and associated buildings to accommodate their exotics. Some of Brown's patrons in Kent exemplified the rise in the fortunes of the business, professional and mercantile classes, even though these same landowners had close connections with the landed aristocracy who wielded strong social and political influence. The Kent sites also re-inforce long-held views that his extraordinary success as a landscape gardener, architect and businessman depended as much upon the support of like-minded contemporaries as it did upon the support of his patrons. Brown's commissions in Kent may not be among the most significant, but they do provide some highly valuable insights which help broaden our understanding of his work.

References
1   Phibbs, pp.246-277 The number of commissions attributed to Brown is based on information compiled by Phibbs where 100% attributions have been made based only on 'accounts (A), correspondence (C) and signed plans or pictures (P).'
2   Remington, p.173
3   Jennings, p.14 The ha-ha was an important landscaping device used by Bridgeman and copied extensively by Brown.
4   Stone, Hooper, Shaw, and Tanner, Journal of the Garden History Society, Summer 2015, p.78

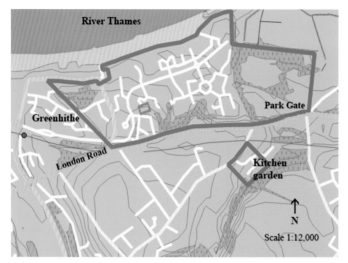

Ingress in today's setting

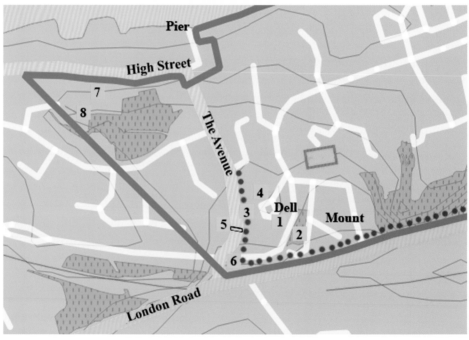

Key features

1. Cave of the Seven Heads
2. Flint Grotto
3. Site of third cave
4. Possible site of Doric temple
5. Bridge over the Avenue
6. Site of Ionic temple
7. Octagonal lookout tower
8. Pagoda - Eagles Nest

☐ Boundary of designed landscape 1760-77
☐ Site of former mansion
●●● Former perimeter path

Ingress: the Contributions of Capability Brown and William Chambers

Ingress lies on the southern bank of the River Thames, immediately to the east of Greenhithe, in a landscape which has changed continuously over the past 500 years. From a farm belonging to the priory of Dartford in the 14th century, the site had become a major chalk quarry a century later, a process which continued to the 19th century and it was the profit from this which allowed a mansion house to be built on the site by 1649.[1]   Dramatic cliffs still form the backdrop to the present 19th century house where for the last 300 years successive owners have acquired more land, enabling them to make major changes to the landscape but, at the same time, making it difficult to discover those which Lancelot 'Capability' Brown carried out between 1763 and 1772. His improvements, which survived into the 19th century, were gradually lost during the 20th century, initially when the park was submerged beneath paper mills and later when the Merchant Navy College was built adjacent to the present house in 1968. By the 21st century the college and mills had gone, and in their place a large housing estate now covers most of the area, the whole process being recorded in an extensive series of archaeological reports over 13 years which have been summarised by Capon.[2]

This chapter is concerned with the work of Brown at Ingress but it soon becomes apparent that another great garden designer and architect, Sir William Chambers (1722-1796), was very much involved not only with the grounds but also in re-building the house. In order to discover what they each did, it is necessary to trace the history of the mansion house and the land on which it was built in 1649, to the house which was finally pulled down in 1833 and replaced by the present building.

The house, depicted by Badeslade in an engraving published by Harris in 1719[3] (fig.1), belonged at that time to Jonathon Smith and is shown to be set on a slope extending from the

Figure 1.
View of Ingress by
Badeslade, 1719
Courtesy: Kent
Archaeological Society

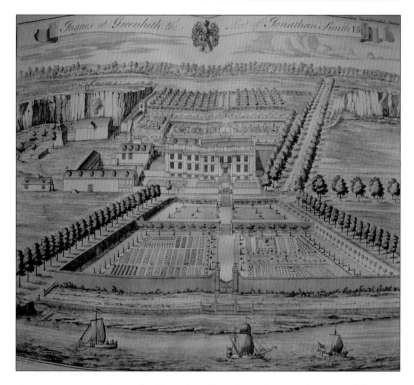

river in the north to the London Road to the south. On either side are severe cliffs below which are signs of active quarrying but, in the midst of this, to the north and south of the house, are formal gardens extending, by means of terraces, the length of the slope. Harris who describes these as 'very pleasing',[4] also states that Jonathon Smith had re-fronted the house.

More detail can be gleaned from a trust deed prepared by William Daniel in 1737[5] for John Carmichael, third Earl of Hyndford, who paid Smith £1130.10s for the house and 21 acres of land. Included in the sale documents is a contemporary survey[6] (fig.2) which correlates well with the 1719 print except in one detail, for it is apparent that the gardens to the north of the house were very much smaller than those depicted by Badeslade, raising the question as to whether those nearest the river were ever laid out in the first place. This area is referred to in the deeds of the same year as the Green and this seems a more suitable description, particularly when comparing it with the later engraving of 1752 by Boydell[7] where it is shown as a grassy slope extending down towards the river.

It was William Ponsonby, the next owner of Ingress, who commissioned the engraving (fig.3) which shows buildings extending from the east and the west of the house, an avenue leading westwards to Greenhithe and the roadway along the river bank. To the west, above Greenhithe, a naval flag is flying and just above the roofline of the village a small tower can be seen.

Ponsonby had bought the estate for £1800 from the Earl of Hyndford in 1748 with the same 21 acres and, in the following year, he entered into a financial arrangement concerning Ingress with George, Lord Anson.[8] Together they bought more land lying to the west of Slaves Alley, today known as the Avenue. It is on this seven acres, called then Little Kiln Cliff and today Eagle Cliff, that Anson's flag, as admiral of the Western squadron and later first lord of the Admiralty, can be seen flying and it is probably his tower, perhaps built as a lookout that is still there today.[9] Although he kept his interest in Ingress, in 1753 Anson bought Moor Park in Hertfordshire and the next year commissioned Brown to make over the grounds there, 10 years before he was to start work at Ingress.

William Ponsonby had made the grand tour from 1736-38 and travelled extensively both in Italy and Turkey from where he had brought back a 'valuable collection' of Roman altars and other artefacts, journeys which are described in detail by

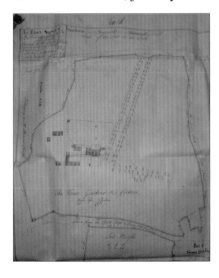

Figure 2. (left)
The survey prepared for the Earl of Hyndford, 1737
Courtesy: The National Archives
Figure 3. (right)
View of Ingress by Boydell, 1752
Courtesy: London Metropolitan Archives

Finnegan who gives a full account of his life and interests.[10]   In the same year in which he set out, Ponsonby had been made a member of the Society of Dilettanti, of which the founder was Thomas Anson, the elder brother of George, and owner of Shugborough.

Following his return to England, Ponsonby, now Lord Duncannon, had married Caroline, the eldest daughter of the third Duke of Devonshire, and the couple lived in London until acquiring Ingress in 1748. Here he set about landscaping the gardens so that his collections might be displayed[11] and he was helped initially by William Atkinson, between 1752-7, who, amongst other things, built a Doric temple.[12] However, it was William Chambers who made the important changes to the landscape.

Chambers had arrived in England in 1755 after pursuing his architectural studies in France and Italy, prior to which he had made three trips to China which had aroused his passion for the Orient. His unique knowledge of China and ability as an architect quickly found him work and, in 1757, he was appointed tutor in architecture to the future George III and architect to Augusta, Dowager Princess of Wales. Chambers designed an Ionic temple for Ponsonby which was sited in a 'hollow of the chalk cliffs' and was very similar to the Temple of Arethusa at Kew which he had completed in 1758.[13]

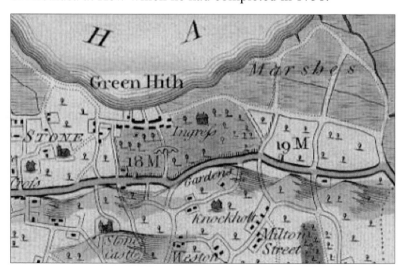

Figure 4.
Part of the hundred of Axtane, from Hasted's map of 1797

26

Figure 5.
View of Greenhithe
looking north and
showing the Eagle's
Nest pagoda

The pleasure ground at Ingress lay to the southwest of the
house and extended westwards across Slaves Alley (now the
Avenue) to Little Kiln Cliff (now Eagle Cliff), the two halves
being connected by a bridge, and totalling seven acres.[14]   The
area nearest the house was known as the Dell and within this
Chambers placed the two temples, the Cave of the Seven
Heads, the Flint Grotto and a third cave; while in the western
part he built the Eagle's Nest, a Chinese pagoda[15] (fig.5).
Some of these features can be seen in the early maps; for
example, the bridge, which is shown on Hasted's map of
1797[16] (fig.4), was still present on the second edition Ordnance
Survey map (1897-1900) but now only the bases of the pillars
can be seen in the Avenue, 100 metres south of the main road.
The Cave of the Seven Heads is still there, tucked under what
was the 19th-century entrance drive, and the Flint Grotto also
remains higher up the same road and opening onto it. Standing
in the present road entering the Dell, it is still possible to see the
shape of the 18th-century landscape despite the later changes
and the building all around. All that remains of the pagoda are
the foundations, set at a now inaccessible point on the cliff.
Buildings were lost when both the temples were sold in 1820
together with garden ornaments which included a pair of lead
sphinxes and caryatids.[17] Chambers' Ionic temple is still to be
seen to this day, no longer at Ingress, but at Cobham Hall just
10km to the southeast, to where it was moved after the sale, and
is now known as Lady Darnley's Gazebo.

The buildings in the pleasure ground seem to have been sited in accordance with Chambers' theories. In his 'Art of Laying Out Gardens', published in 1757, he describes the creation of a landscape which, while still natural, would be improved by judicious planting and the placing of artefacts, with grottos which could be cut 'into a variety of apartment' or, perhaps, a mixture of buildings artfully placed so that they might be viewed singularly or as a whole. He considered that paths should lead from one place to the next in such a way that the visitor is guided without being aware of the fact.[18]

An inventory of 1772[19] shows that statues, columns, vases and bas reliefs were arranged both around the pleasure ground and in the follies which were well equipped with tables and chairs and were clearly used as much for picnics as meditation. There were nine bas reliefs set in the walls of the bridge and in one of the caves 'twelve pieces of brass cannon', presumably a legacy of Lord Anson. The bridge and temple are described adjacent to each other in the inventory, suggesting they were close together, the latter perhaps on the cliff to the east of the Avenue.

Disaster befell Ponsonby, by then Lord Bessborough, in 1760 when his family were struck down by a terrible contagion, possibly cholera. Not only his wife, Caroline, but all his children save two daughters and his youngest son died and as a result he could no longer bear to live at Ingress. He moved away to Roehampton where he commissioned Chambers to build him a Palladian villa, Parkstead House (also known as Manresa House).[20]

Ingress was sold and the estate, house and contents bought for £5249 by John Calcraft (1726-1772),[21] an army agent, a political fixer and an opportunist. Receiving his initial post through the Marquess of Granby and his subsequent advancement as a protégé of Henry Fox[22] who was possibly a cousin, he obtained lucrative positions in the war office which enabled him to buy extensive estates in Dorset and Lincolnshire. He had already leased Holwood House in Keston where £600 had been spent on creating a garden with the help of his mistress, George Ann Bellamy, who entertained the 'political junto' for him,[23] a group made up of the Dukes of

Marlborough, Bedford and, occasionally, Cumberland, together with Henry Fox and Charles Townsend.[24]   Purchasing Ingress was Calcraft's opportunity to promote himself.

Initially buying the 21 acres around the house and the seven acres of Little Kiln Cliff through his younger brother, Thomas, John Calcraft set out to buy other lands nearby and by the time of his death 12 years later, he had acquired 181 acres. Only 18 miles from London on the main Dover Road, Ingress was equally accessible by the river and was furnished in a suitably opulent manner to enable him to continue entertaining in the grand manner.[25]   Calcraft used this to further his political ambitions becoming Member of Parliament for Calne in 1766 and, two years later, Member for Rochester.

He was well able to afford the best and while continuing to employ Chambers, principally to alter the house, at the same time brought in Brown to alter Bessborough's park and to create a further landscape on the additional land he had purchased to the east and north of the main house. No details of the contracts other than the amounts which he paid Brown survive: £500 in 1763-4 and a further £500 in 1771;[26] in addition, he paid him a further £1800 for his work at Leeds Abbey, another property in Kent which Calcraft had purchased in 1765. Additionally, over the same period, he paid Chambers £1000 in 1771[27] with £74[28] still outstanding a year later. Although there is no documentation to say how this money was spent, Fisher's comments in 1776, only four years after Calcraft's death, that the improvements to the west of the house were made by Lord Bessborough (Chambers) and the rest by Calcraft (Brown), provide the clue. In addition, Fisher stated that Calcraft had 'removed a great bank of earth on the south side and by this means made it more airy and cheerful. The old kitchen garden was upon this spot but Mr Calcraft enclosed a large piece of ground for this use on the other side of the road, within which he erected a hot house'.[29] Further evidence from near contemporary maps can be used to show changes to the planting in the park which seem typical of Brown's work.

The Andrews, Dury and Herbert map of 1769 appears to show the landscape created by Lord Bessborough, perhaps surveyed two or three years after Calcraft had acquired it and before Brown had started work (fig.6). The southern garden of the Badeslade drawing is still there but the orchard has been replaced by a planting of trees or shrubs extending south-westwards below the cliffs which are now tree covered, the appearance extending across the Avenue (Slaves Alley) to the western garden reflecting the changes made by Chambers to the pleasure ground.

If this is compared with the Ordnance Survey drawings made 30 years later[30] (fig.7) and supplemented with naval surveys of 1810/11, an idea of the improvements made by Brown can be appreciated. Neither Calcraft's heir nor the subsequent owner, Henry Woodhouse Disney Roebuck, appear to have carried out more work on the landscape, the latter being more interested in sailing, and thus Brown's landscape had had a chance to mature when it was pictured by Miss Havelock in 1812 (fig.8) and in a further print of 1821 (fig.13).

Figure 6. (left) Ingress and Greenhithe, based on the Andrews, Dury and Herbert map of 1769. The boundary shows the land bought by Calcraft from Lord Bessborough *Courtesy: Kent History and Library Centre*
Figure 7. (right) Ingress from the Ordnance Survey drawing of 1799 *Courtesy: British Library*

In the drawings of 1799, the formal straight lines of the avenues have gone; Brown has replaced these with clumps between the house and the Thames, allowing tantalising vistas across the river towards the coast of Essex. He did not have to divert any part of the Thames, the panorama was already there and his task was twofold, to frame the picture and to create an equally elegant reverse view of the house when seen from the river.

By preserving trees to the west of the house and adding a sinuous line eastwards, he has emphasised Chambers' new façade to the house and at the same time hidden the outbuildings which can just be seen under the fringe of trees.

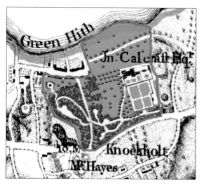

During the removal of the formal avenue between the house and the river, Brown may possibly, as was his practice, have left some of the existing mature trees to create the clumps. As well as framing views, plantings were used to screen unwelcome intrusions, in this case the working quarry to the east of the house which has been hidden by a double row of trees (fig.9).

Calcraft continued to buy up more arable and marshland eastwards towards Northfleet. It was here, perhaps during a subsequent visit, on rising ground known as the Downs and over which the drive led eastwards to the cottages near the Park Gate[31] on the London Road (fig. 9), that Brown planted a broad stand of trees and a clump to give the effect of hangers, visible from the park and house and providing a perspective to the

Figure 8. (above) Ingress from a drawing by Miss Helen Havelock, 1812
Figure 9. (below) Map of Ingress, 1811. Part of the plan of the proposed grand navel arsenal is shown to the east. This was never built
Courtesy: The National Archives

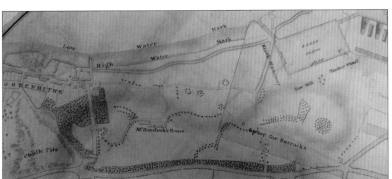

view.[32] Such planting is typical of Brown, producing a dramatic change to the landscape which was only fully realised many years later when the trees had matured. Here on the Thames, as well as the view, wildfowling must have been a major additional attraction.

The Ordnance Survey drawing of 1799 and the map of 1811 confirm planting to the west of the house round the Dell and, also, along the southern boundary of the gardens on the London Road, perhaps a legacy of Lord Bessborough, but the drawing also shows an additional feature. A perimeter pathway can be seen running south on the ridge of land immediately east of the Avenue which allowed views across the Dell, in which almost certainly lay the Doric temple perhaps known as the Mausoleum,[33] eastwards to the Grotto and the Cave of Seven Heads. The path continued to lead southwards, past the third cave, to the bridge where a choice could be made to cross west to Eagle Cliff or turn east, past the second temple and along the cliff top alongside the London Road.

Here, in 1998, the Debois Landscape Group found the remains of large boles of holm oaks, a favourite tree of Brown's[34] and a further feature, no longer accessible, which was a viewing platform looking northwards across both the Dell and the house to the river. A little further on, the 18th century wanderer would have emerged from the trees to reach a mound, probably another lookout point noted by the researchers,[35] before coming to the junction with Knockhall Road and the kitchen garden. From here the more adventurous could have completed a round trip, returning northwards by Love Lane to the east-west drive across the park and thence to the house while enjoying views to the river. This was perhaps also the route used for bringing produce to the house from the garden.

The viewing platform looked down on the gardens to the south side of the house from where it appears that Brown cleared the large bank of earth making the prospect from the house 'more airy and cheerful' and at the same time, as Fisher noted, removed the 'old kitchen garden'. This area was included in the inventory of 1772 in which entries suggest that not all the earlier formal garden was removed. Known as the 'back front' it contained two groups of buildings, one called the Mount which contained not only bas reliefs and ancient vases but also 'at the top an engine for raising the water in buckets'.[36] Could this be the two-storey building shown in Badeslade's 1719 print and marked on the Earl of Hyndford's 1737 survey (fig.2) in the south-east corner, and which may have contained the small hot air furnace excavated by Capon and his colleagues in 2004?[37] The inventory further stated that close by were two engine houses, one of which contained a well and pump while the other had a 'horse engine' with pipes for raising water both to a reservoir in the pleasure ground and to the house[38] but there is nothing to suggest by whom they were built. They too were excavated by Capon who found a large well, securely

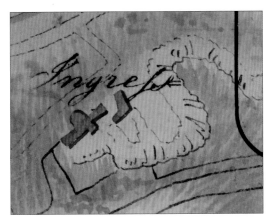

Figure 10.
Part of the naval survey of Ingress, 1810, showing the formation of the cliffs and the coach house block, to the east of the main house, which later became the site of James Harmer's new house in the 19th century
Courtesy: The National Archives

mortared and over 30 metres deep, with machinery, suggesting that water had been drawn by horse power into a series of branching slate covered drains.[39] These were later used in the 19th century to carry water to the greenhouses, and the building came to be known as the Well House;[40] it is now buried beneath a road.

To the east of the house was a large building containing stables, a coach house and servants' living quarters.[41] The 1810/11 maps reveal a similar layout to that shown in the 1719 Badeslade print; no pleasure ground is apparent in this area and, in addition, there is no recorded evidence of artefacts in the 1772 inventory. It was only later, in the 19th century, that a new pleasure ground was laid out here by James Harmer, immediately to the south of his new house, built on the site of the former coach block, and consisting of the follies created for him: the Granary, the Monks' Well, the Lovers' Arch, the tunnels and the interconnecting paths. Forming most of today's remaining historic designed landscape, these are described in the historic building listings[42] and are open to the public.

One noticeable feature of all the surveys of Ingress is the absence of any entrance onto the London Road; the principal entrance to the western side of the park is directly from Greenhithe at the northern end of the Avenue where visitors coming by water would also have arrived.[43] The map of 1769 (fig.6) shows that the former south entrance had been closed off and the drive shortened. By 1811, this becomes a path curving round the southern end of the Dell, more in line with the later 19th-century drive, to lead the walker through the pleasure ground, past Chambers' caves and the temples, towards the bridge across the Avenue, meeting the perimeter path at this point. Emphasising features in this way could have been the work of either Brown or Chambers who both approved of curved paths used for this purpose.

But there seems little doubt about who designed the kitchen garden for Calcraft. Fisher had noted the removal of the 'old kitchen garden' to the south of the house and its replacement with another on the other side of the road; this is immediately apparent on comparing the Andrew's map (fig.6) and the 1799 Ordnance Survey drawing where the new garden is shown laid out along the southeast side of what is now Knockhall Road and from which it was separated by a belt of trees and shrubs. The drawing shows that it was correctly orientated to receive maximum sun, the whole very similar in layout and design to that which Brown had created at Ashburnham Place in East

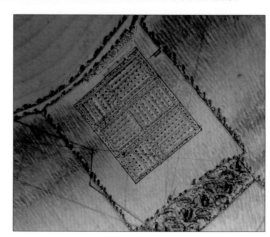

Figure 11.
The kitchen garden,
from a survey of 1810
Courtesy: National
Archives

Sussex at about the same time. Brown had a very definite interest in creating designs in which could be grown the exotic fruit and vegetables demanded by his clients; skills which were to be scathingly dismissed by Chambers, in his essay of 1772, as merely the 'culture of salads'.[44] The garden is described in the sales details of 1790 as follows:

> *'The Kitchen Garden divided into parts which contain both the outside Borders about 6 acres and judiciously placed on the adjoining ffarm to a full South aspect, the walls near 14 feet high part of Each have Flues and richly Cloathed with the Choisest of ffruit Trees, a well constructed propagating and succession house near 90 feet long, a Fruiting and Tool House Melon Ground etc.'*[45]

From the detailed inventory taken two months after John Calcraft's death in 1772, it is apparent that each hothouse had two stoves and there was a fully equipped tool shed. In addition, there was a house on the site which seems to have been little more than one room but fully furnished together with a scullery and an additional men's room complete with bedding. Because the inventory would have only been concerned with objects that had some value, there is no record of building structures as such, and so in the garden only 5 bell glasses, 23 hand glasses and 40 melon lights are listed, but there were two lead statues, one of Mercury and one of Fame.[46] These two figures were sometimes used to represent war and peace and it is significant that they had been placed there as the Seven Years War had ended in 1763, perhaps as a compliment to William Pitt (1708-78), the first earl of Chatham and the statesman who had led the country through this period.

Details of the garden can be seen in the survey of 1810 (fig.11).[47] Shown to be still a walled garden in an aerial photograph of 1946 (fig.12),[48] it is now buried under a housing estate, Ingress Gardens, with no trace of Brown's work remaining.

Having built on Lord Bessborough's work and design, and with the expertise of Brown and Chambers, Calcraft had achieved

Figure 12.
Aerial photographs
of the kitchen garden
created by Brown
Courtesy: Kent
Historic Environment
Record

sufficient further improvements in his 12 years of occupancy for Ingress to merit the following description by Fisher in 1772, the year in which Calcraft died.

> *'The house is very convenient, and the gardens*
> *beautifully romantic: from a spacious and elegant room*
> *at the west end of the house, as well as from various*
> *parts of the gardens, the eye is entertained with views*
> *of the river and the Essex shore, that are perfectly*
> *enchanting: and upon the whole it is one of the most*
> *delightful spots on the bank of the Thames.'*[49]

Some further notes from the auction details of 1788 held by Mr Christie at his Great Room in Pall Mall include the following:

> *'The house and distant picturesque views, render this*
> *one of the most distinguished spots in the Kingdom,*
> *consist of a Commodious House seated on a most*
> *Verdant Lawn fringed with Plantations dispersed*
> *with a Taste superlative Interspersed with Marble and*
> *Stone Inrichments of Grecian Workmanship, Temples,*
> *Grottos, Vases, Mausoleum etc'.*[50]

36

Only 42 years old, John Calcraft died quite suddenly in August 1772, leaving his eldest son, also John, by his second acknowledged mistress, Elizabeth Bride, as his heir.[51] John was only seven years old at the time of his father's death and he and his siblings were initially brought up at Ingress but later moved to Rempstone on Elizabeth's marriage to Charles Lefebure (1773). The care of the gardens was left to George Sharpe, Calcraft's trusted servant, and Ingress was leased out before being sold to Henry Woodhouse Disney Roebuck[52] (not John Disney Roebuck as usually stated), a keen yachtsman and noted mariner.[53] It was he who was responsible for bringing the case in Chancery against various members of the Calcraft family, resulting in preservation of some of the records of the estate in 1790. Dying in 1796, Ingress passed to Roebuck's son, another Henry Roebuck, who appears to have had no interest in it, returning to the family roots at Ickford in Buckinghamshire and a career in the army.[54] The estate was sold to William Havelock and it was his daughter, Helen, who made the drawing for the engraving of 1812. After prolonged negotiation with the Admiralty, this entrepreneur from Sunderland managed to sell the estate to the Crown in 1813 for an agreed price of £45,000[55] to be developed as a 'grand naval arsenal'. The house was not demolished by the Crown, as sometimes stated, but continued to be tenanted until it was sold at auction, in 1831[56] to James Harmer, lawyer and alderman from London, who built the present house, slightly to the east on the site of the former coach houses and still there today, while at the same time embarking on another major alteration to the landscape. In letters to Fanny Talboys, his niece, Harmer records moving 100,000 cartloads of chalk to make improvements to the north of his new house in order to create a sloping terrace and view to the river edge where the chalk was used to build up the river bank.[57] This is one example of the many major engineering works carried out by successive owners of Ingress which continue to the present day, and it is this continual change which makes it so difficult to work out the sequence of landscape changes.

The only constant features at Ingress over the last 300 years are the river and the chalk cliffs; during that time the land between has been constantly re-shaped. All that is left of the landscape

Figure 13.
Engraving by Cooke,
1821
Courtesy: Kent
Archaeological Society

of Brown and Chambers are a few documents, the remnants of a bridge, the line of a drive, two caves in the shadow of the Dell, a lookout and a single vista northwards to the Thames and the coast of Essex beyond, though this is no longer framed by trees but by terraces of houses. And one last question: did the works which the two great men carried out at Ingress over nearly 10 years, fuel their differences?

Chambers had started work on Kew Garden in 1757 for Augusta, Dowager Princess of Wales, and in 1765 Brown commenced changes at Richmond Lodge for George III, resulting in two very different gardens which are shown in a survey of 1771[58] lying side by side. The rather controlled landscape of Chambers, perhaps over-populated with buildings, contrasts with the more relaxed and open landscape of Brown but together, in some ways, they resemble the style of the changes which each had made at Ingress over the same period although on a smaller scale: the temple and pagoda versus the broad vistas framed by trees.

38

In 1768, Chambers had failed to gain the commission at Claremont which Lord Clive awarded to Brown. This may have added to his resentment which seems to have come to a head in 1772 with the publication of his essay on oriental gardening,[59] in the preface to which he made derogatory remarks about Brown's methods, comments which, it would appear, Brown never answered. The only response came from the Rev. William Mason, the following year, in a satirical poem[60] which did nothing to enhance Chambers' reputation but rather made him a laughing stock. Despite his enduring eminence as an architect, he never achieved the same reputation as a creator of gardens although some of his ideas for dramatic landscapes came to be used in the Picturesque movement at the end of 18th century as fashions changed and the never ending search for something new continued. Capability Brown, on the other hand, will always be revered as the English landscaper par excellence.

Figure 14.
Ingress Abbey in the 21st century, seen from the memorial to the Incorporated Thames Nautical Training College, HMS Worcester. The memorial stands on the edge of the River Thames at the same place from which the images of Ingress were composed in 1812 and 1821 (see figs. 8 and 13)

39

References

1   Hasted (1972 edition), vol.2, pp.399-421
2   Capon, vol.129, p.1
3   Harris, History of Kent, pp.308-9
4   Ibid. p.309
5   The National Archives (TNA), The Crown Estate Commissioners and Predecessors, CRES 38/361, 1660-1746
6   Ibid.
7   Boydell, A View of Lord Duncannon's House in the County of Kent, engraving, 1752, City of London Corporation
8   TNA, CRES 38/362, 1747-80. William Ponsonby (1704-1793), Viscount Duncannon and second earl of Bessborough. Lord George Anson (1697-1762) circumnavigated the world between 1740-44 and became First Lord of the Admiralty in 1751.
9   Listed entries under the Planning (Listed Buildings and Conservation Areas) Act 1990 as amended for its special architectural or historic interest, No. 475253
10   Finnegan, vol.8, pp.12-43
11   Ibid.
12   West Sussex Record Office, Index of Correspondents in the Bessborough Manuscripts
13   Harris, Sir William Chambers, Architect to George III, pp.1-9
14   Kent History and Library Centre (KHLC), Andrews, Dury and Herbert map, 1769, EK/U20/1 Dorset History Centre (DHC). Roebuck v Calcraft copy bill in Chancery, Ryder of Rempstone Archive D/RWR: L6, 1790
15   Tomblesome, W. Greenhithe, Kent, steel engraving, 1830
16   Hasted (1972 edition), vol.2
17   Advertisement, Times, 24 October 1820, p.4
18   Chambers, Designs of Chinese Buildings, Furniture, Dresses, Machines and Utensils, pp.14-19
19   TNA, Lucas v Calcraft; Inventory of a House Belonging to John Calcraft, Deceased, Chancery, C104/242, Inventory, 1772, fol. 11
20   Finnegan, vol.8, pp.10-11
21   TNA, CRES 38/362, 1747-80
22   John Manners, Marquis of Granby (1721-1770), MP for Grantham 1742 and distinguished soldier. Henry Fox (1705-1774), politician and contemporary of William Pitt, Earl of Chatham; he was made Lord Holland in 1763.
23   Bellamy, vol.2, p.226
24   Ibid., vol.3, p.119
25   TNA, C104/242, Inventory, 1772, fol. 5-6
26   Willis, vol.27, p.385
27   Harris, Sir William Chambers, p.175
28   Ibid. p.212
29   Fisher, The Kentish Traveller's Companion, p.42
30   Ordnance Survey Drawing, Dartford, 1799. OSD 129 (Kent County Council, Heritage Environment Record)
31   DHC, Roebuck v Calcraft, D/RWR: L6
32   TNA, MPHH 1/539, Plan of a Naval Arsenal at Greenhithe and Northfleet, 1811
33   TNA, C104/242, Inventory, 1772, As well as containing nine bas reliefs, there was 'an antique figure on top', fol. 11
34   Debois Landscape Group, Ingress Abbey, Greenhithe, Kent, 1998, p.6

35   Ibid. Follies and Field Notes, no. 33, Clifftop views (surviving), perhaps Mount Nod, OS map, 1864. Brown often created mounds from the spoil of excavation.
36   TNA, C104/242, Inventory, 1772, fol. 11
37   AOC Archaeology Group, Results of Archaeological Excavation at Ingress Abbey (2004), Building 1, An 18th Century Hot Air Furnace, p.46
38   TNA, C104/242, Inventory, 1772, fol.11
39   AOC Archaeology Group, Building 7, The Well House, pp.51-2
40   Ordnance Survey map, 25ins, first edition, 1864
41   TNA, C104/242, Inventory, 1772, fol. 9
42   Listed building entries, Nos. 1362089, 1362090 and 1, 1245694 and 5
43   The Ordnance Survey drawings and naval survey maps suggest that there may have been a smaller subsidiary entrance halfway along the Avenue, directly west of the house, crossing to Eagle Cliff.
44   Chambers, A Dissertation on Oriental Gardening, p.iii
45   DHC, Roebuck v Calcraft, D/RWR: L6
46   TNA, C104/242, Inventory, 1772, fol. 10
47   TNA, Land adjacent to a proposed naval establishment, 1810, MR 1/1347
48   Kent County Council Heritage Conservation Group, Ingress Abbey, aerial photograph, 1946
49   Fisher, The History and Antiquities of Rochester, p.298
50   DHC, Roebuck v Calcraft, D/RWR: L6
51   DHC, Copy will of John Calcraft, D/RWR: E24
52   TNA, CRES 38/363, 1748-1818
53   The Gentleman's Magazine and Historical Chronicle, Obituary, April 1796, vol. 66 part 1, p.384
54   The United Service Journal, vol.1829, part II, p.258
55   Caird Library, Royal Naval Maritime Museum, Letter from William Havelock to Edward Hall – Secretary at Navy Office, ADM/BP/33a, 1813
56   Gravesend Library, Freehold Estates, Hive and Swanscombe, sales details, 6th July 1831
57   KHLC, Letters from JW Harmer of Ingress Abbey to Fanny, U2198/C/1, 1841
58   Brown, p.224
59   Chambers, A Dissertation on Oriental Gardening, pp.i-xi
60   Mason, pp.5-16

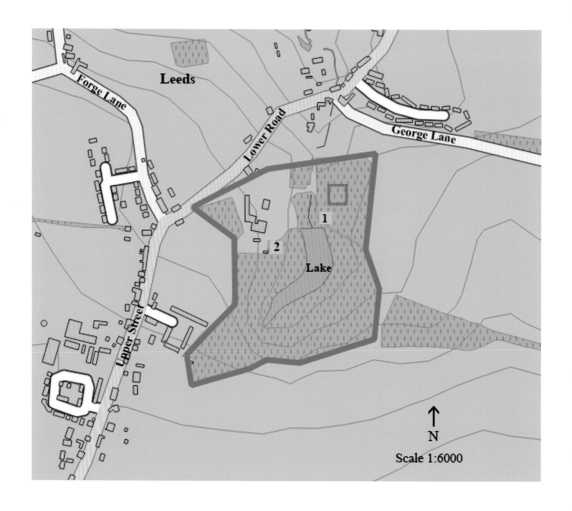

Leeds Abbey in today's setting

Key features

1. Slype
2. Pigeon houses

Boundary of designed landscape 1770-72

Site of former mansion and priory

Leeds Abbey: A Hidden Brown Landscape

Immediately west of Leeds Castle in Kent lies the site of the priory which had been founded in the 14th century and which was dismantled after the Dissolution. The land was granted to Anthony St Leger in 1550 and later sold to William Covert whose son built the house which came to be known as Leeds Abbey and which is shown in the Badeslade drawing published in 1719. The gardens are shown to be very formally arranged, following the fashion of the time, but only forty six years later, the then owner John Calcraft commissioned Lancelot 'Capability' Brown to sweep this away and replace it with an informal lake and parkland. It is this landscape which is still present today though shrouded in scrub and woodland which in turn hides the remains of the buried priory.

Robert de Crevequer had endowed the priory of the black canons of the Order of St Augustine in 1367, 'giving them a site to build their church upon with other convenient buildings, the former to be dedicated in honour of St Mary and St Nicholas'[1] but by the reign of Henry VII the community was deep in debt. This time they were relieved by James Goldwell, bishop of Norwich, who founded a chantry in the south part of the nave and who, for this generosity, came to be looked on as the second founder. By 1534, the clear revenues of the priory were £362.7s, which was considerably more than Michelham in Sussex at £191 but very much less than Merton in Surrey at £960. In this year, the prior, Arthur St Leger, signed the Act of Supremacy and five years later the priory was surrendered to the Crown.[2]

Shortly afterwards his relative, Anthony St Leger, was granted a lease of the priory lands in the parish of Leeds for 21 years but, at the same time, the king ordered the priory and all the buildings within the precinct to be pulled down. Eventually, the site of the priory with its demesne lands was settled on St Leger, a total of 229 acres, to be held in capite of the king. The remainder of the estates were settled on the dean and chapter of Rochester, a new foundation created by Henry VIII.[3]

For the 50 years following the death of Sir Anthony, as he had become, the estate passed from the St Legers to the Nordens and then to William Covert. Hasted says that Covert's son, who lived there, 'new built the front of the house, as it now remains, and rebuilt much of the rest of the ancient buildings of the priory'[4] and that, at the time of writing, the initials, WC and the date 1598, were still to be seen but he does not comment on the grounds.

Ten years later (1608), the estate, now known as Leeds Abbey, was bought by Sir William Meredith whose family remained in ownership for the next 150 years during which time they acquired more land from the St Leger family.[5] By 1742, some 750 acres (304 hectares) lying immediately west of the Leeds Castle estate and in the parishes of Leeds and Langley were in their possession, the house and gardens extended to 30 acres (12 hectares).[6]

A succession of Merediths followed each other, the first baronet of Leeds Abbey, another William, being created in 1622. The second, Richard, was a lawyer, Member of Parliament for Kent

**Figure 1.
Leeds Abbey (looking south) as shown in Harris, History of Kent, 1719** *Courtesy: Kent Archaeological Society*

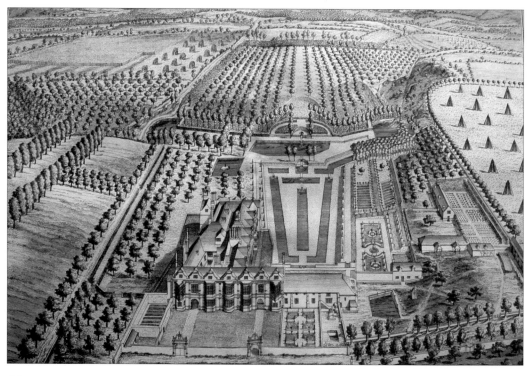

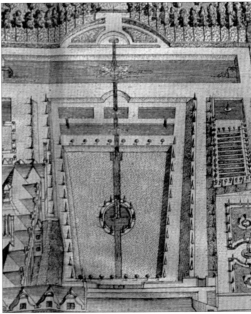

in the Second Protectorate Parliament of 1656 and member for Sandwich in 1659, who died in 1679 leaving six sons, three of whom succeeded in turn: William, Richard and Roger. None of them produced an heir and so the baronetcy died with the last, Sir Roger, in 1738.[7]

Following Sir Richard's death in 1679, a detailed inventory of the house had been carried out, room by room.[8] This is the house whose front was new built by Covert and is shown in a plate drawn by Badeslade (fig.1), engraved by Kip and included in Harris's History of Kent (1719) being dedicated to Roger Meredith, not yet baronet.[9] However another version exists, dedicated to Sir Richard Meredith who was Sir Roger's older brother and who died in 1723. The latter is probably the older version and shows a different layout to the central part of the garden. Sir Richard had been declared lunatic in 1681[10] and, presumably, was incapable of managing his affairs. As it was customary for the owner to pay the expense of preparing the plate, it was probably Roger who paid the bill for the version in Harris, only assuming his title four years later.

Badeslade's plates, which look south to the greensand ridge, only differ in the arrangement of the water features in the

Figure 2.
The water features in the two plates showing the garden in Sir Richard's ownership (left) and then in Roger Meredith's (right)
Courtesy: Kent Archaeological Society

45

central part of the garden (fig.2); a half octagonal pool in the earlier layout has been replaced by a larger rectangular area of water and the three canals, running north to the house through a sunken garden, have been reduced to a single central one. The house, unchanged in the later plate, has an older section to the west of the 'new' front and this probably contained the domestic quarters described in the inventory of 1679. The southern part of the building complex contained a dairy, brewhouse, laundry, granary, coach house and stables. To the west are shown farm buildings and the pigeon houses, one dating from medieval times and the other built at the same time as the house.

Following the death of Sir Roger Meredith in 1738, Leeds Abbey passed to his niece, Susanna, who continued to live there remaining unmarried. Legal complications and the lack of a direct heir resulted in the estate passing through several hands before being bought by John Calcraft in 1765, and it was he who brought in Brown to re-landscape the garden.

Calcraft had made a fortune first as a pay clerk to the War Office, a post he had obtained through the influence of the Marquess of Granby, and then as an agent to the army. He was already owner of Ingress, near Dartford, which he had bought in 1760 and where both Brown and Sir William Chambers were already working for him by 1765 and were to continue to do so until Calcraft's death in 1772. Through his army connections, his wealth and the patronage he had received from Granby and also Henry Fox, he knew many of the leading politicians and seems to have been involved in the political plotting and change of government on the accession of George III. Calcraft used these connections to further a career in politics becoming Member of Parliament first for Calne and then, in 1768, for Rochester.[11] So it is not very surprising to find, in a letter (see opposite) to William Pitt, Earl of Chatham, from Calcraft, references to Lord Bute and to Mr Brown. However, it does raise the question about how often Brown was used by his employers to act as a go-between.

It is not at all clear why Calcraft bought Leeds Abbey. The house was a long way from London, quite old and judging by the inventory far from convenient and yet, following his death, his family were given the choice of living either at Leeds or at Ingress, implying that he was well satisfied with Brown's work at both. The work at Leeds had cost Calcraft £1800: entries in Brown's account book show that the sums of £300 and £500 were paid to him in 1771 and a further £1000 paid the next year by Calcraft's executors, following his premature death.[13] But the improvements were not just Brown's work, for Henry Holland was paid £55.10s.1d for wood carving carried out in the house on his behalf by Henry Wood.[14] These accounts are detailed with those for Valence where Holland was also carrying out work for Brown at about the same time.

The amounts paid to Brown at Leeds were nearly twice that paid at Ingress and with lack of further documentation, it is necessary to interpret the only other evidence available which comes from the appearance of the land today and the historic maps. The earliest is that of Andrews, Dury and Herbert, published in 1769[15] (fig.3) but probably surveyed some years earlier, which records a landscape which corresponds to Badeslade's drawings. It was the formal arrangement of gardens to the south of the house which Brown removed during Calcraft's ownership. This change is revealed in the Ordnance Survey drawings[16] made almost thirty years later (fig.4) which show that the formal, enclosed water features have been replaced by an open landscape shelving from all sides towards a central lake curving to the southwest, fed by springs to the

John Calcraft to the earl of Chatham
Leeds Abbey, Friday evening, May 17, 1771
My dear Lord,
When I had the honour of writing to your Lordship on Tuesday, I was much oppressed with pain and weakness that I scarce knew what I wrote; the attack was most violent though short. It has left me much reduced; but by great care, I hope in a few days to be able personally to express my warmest acknowledgments to your Lordship's and Lady Chatham's obliging attention to one, advised to gain strength, which added to Mr Brown's summons, who is really exerting himself, brought me for two days to this place, which he will much improve. He talks of calling on your Lordship tomorrow: he is full of zeal and projects for Lord Bute on his return: amongst the foremost, is a plan of union with your Lordship. His wish seems to lead him to persuade me to promote this undertaking; but after replying, that Lord Bute and his friends might some years ago have found proper protection from your Lordship, had they confided, I declined ever again becoming a negotiator. Ill able to write as I really am, this seemed proper for me to notify..............Let me entreat your Lordship to believe me your ever obliged, affectionate, and faithful friend and servant, John Calcraft.[12]

south and contained by a dam at the northern end. The lake is surrounded by grassland which at first sight appears to have few features save for a row of trees to the west of the lake and a large clump directly to the south. However, these drawings were probably made within 25 years of the completion of Brown's scheme and many of the trees which he planted may not have been big enough to record.

The building of the dam must have been expensive; some 40 metres across, composed of ragstone and including some remaining stones from the priory, it not only held the water back in the main lake which is some 200 metres long, but also had to control the water supply to the mill pond lying to the north and thus to the mill in the village below. The appearance of the landscape would have been simplified from the complex formality of the early 18th century layout and, in some ways, returned to much earlier times when the monks would have had fish ponds to feed the priory.

Figure 3. (left)
The formal gardens as recorded on the map of Andrews, Dury and Herbert, 1769
Courtesy: Kent History and Library Centre

Figure 4. (right)
Brown's landscape as recorded on the Ordnance Survey surveyor's drawing of 1797
Courtesy: British Library

On the rising ground to the west of the lake were the pigeon houses which Brown probably left in order to provide a feature on the horizon. The two buildings appear as one in the 1719 Badeslade plate, but Caiger suggests that Brown removed part of the masonry between them so that they appeared as two. At the same time he presumably inserted the present windows to

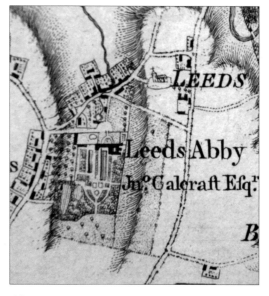
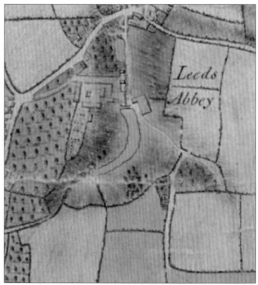

the north and the east and rendered them with mortar giving the appearance of stone quoins and making the building look like a chapel (fig.5), the name by which it came to be known.[17] Beyond the pigeon houses, to the west, seems to have been an area of cultivation, perhaps the same kitchen garden visible in the Badeslade plate of 1719 with an orchard further to the west. Between the pigeon houses and the lake is a slope extending southwards but it is not apparent what is growing on this, although, later, the first edition of the Ordnance Survey of 1868 shows it to be orchard. Did Brown suggest this? Seen from the house, a slope of cherry blossom rising westwards from the tree fringed lake to outline the chapel would have provided a dramatic view in keeping with the surrounding countryside.

The Ordnance Survey map of 1868[18] (fig.6) also shows that other tree planting recorded on the Ordnance Survey 1797 drawing has matured; all are deciduous except for one conifer, probably a Scots pine, on the eastern boundary, which appears in a photograph of 1911[19] and was still there in 1970. Brown frequently used this species for contrast and, here, it would have provided an eye-catcher to the east even though it would

Figure 5.
A photograph of the two pigeon houses published in 1911

49

Figure 6.
First edition
Ordnance Survey
map, 1866
Courtesy: Kent History
and Library Centre

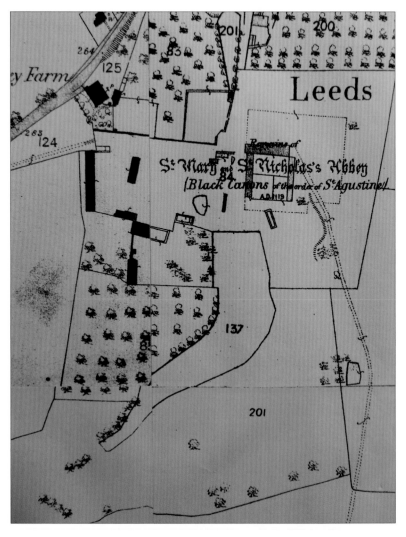

have been many years before it could assume this role. It
is easy to forget when looking at Brown's landscapes today
that he was planting for the future and would never see them
himself in maturity.

At Leeds Abbey, Brown's work probably came to be
appreciated by very few people because John Calcraft died
suddenly in 1772. His heir, also John, was only seven years
old at the time, while his mother, Elizabeth McBride chose
to live at Ingress. The estate was subsequently managed by
Calcraft's executors who included his brother, Thomas, but it
seems to have quickly fallen into dilapidation and by 1787,

Figure 7.
The lake at Leeds Abbey looking south from the dam in July 2015

when the subject of a case in Chancery, the house was said to be 'worth little more than keeping in repair'.[20] A memorial in the parish church at Leeds was said to have recorded that it was pulled down shortly afterwards in 1790.[21] The lands were subsequently purchased by the Wykeham-Martin family of Leeds Castle[22] for agricultural use before being sold to the present owners, the Rochester Bridge Trust.

Today (fig.7) the landscape of Brown and Calcraft is still there, albeit now covered with scrub and trees; the bowl of ground sloping on all sides to the central lake is now heavily fringed with reeds, but clear water flows over the dam at the northern end to the site of the mill below. The lake is still big enough to imagine how it could have looked unencumbered by its scrub-covered banks, and from the dam the outline of the pigeon house can just be seen through the overgrowth of trees. None of the trees are old enough to be survivors from

51

the 18th century but there are many young trees of oak, beech, sweet chestnut and scots pine which could be descendants of the first planting. The only farm buildings surviving from the 18th century or earlier are the two pigeon houses and a few walls incorporated into the present day (20th century) barns which are now, in turn, disused. The small building just to the northeast of the lake and known as the 'slype' is the only remaining structure of the medieval priory above ground. The rest of Robert de Crevequer's foundation lies buried below the surface where it was returned after the excavations in the 1970s.[23] Visit Leeds Abbey in the summer and it is almost impossible to make anything out, but visit in winter when the stinging nettles and brambles have died back and suddenly the ghost of the landscape is there, just as it was depicted in the Ordnance Survey drawings of 1797; only the house is missing.

References

1   Dugdale, vol.6, part 1, p.215
2   Ibid. pp.218, 245, 496
3   Hasted (1972 edition),vol.5, p.478-502
4   Ibid. p.495
5   Ibid. pp.478-502
6   Kent History and Library Centre, Brabourne manuscripts, U274 T89
7   Burke, p.426
8   Kent History and Library Centre, U274 F6
9   Harris, History of Kent, p.176
10   The National Archives, Chancery, Inquisition of Lunacy, C211/16/M7, 1681
11   Courtney and Woodland
12   Taylor and Pringle, Correspondence of William Pitt, Earl of Chatham, vol.4, pp. 172-9
13   Royal Horticultural Society Lindley Libraries, The Account Book of Lancelot Brown, 1764-1788 (unpublished manuscript), p.83
14   Henry Holland's 'Price Books', Soane archives, case 128, Sir John Soane's Museum, London
15   Andrews, Dury, and Herbert, A Topographical Map of the County of Kent (London, 1769)
16   Ordnance Survey Drawing, Maidstone, 1797, OSD 117 (British Library)
17   Caiger, vol.89, pp.36-41
18   Ordnance Survey map, 25" to 1 mile, first edition, 1868, sheets 43/9, 43/10, 43/13 and 43/14
19   Fielding, pp.239-51
20   Dorset History Centre, Ryder of Rempstone Archive, D/RWR: L6, 1790
21   Brayley, vol.8, p.1225
22   Kent Archaeological Society, Leeds, nr. Maidstone, Tithe Award Schedule signed 4th May 1844
23   Tester, vol.94, pp.75-98

Valence in today's setting

Key features

1. Site of former kitchen garden
2. Site of former cascade
3. Lime Avenue
4. Valence School
5. Middle Lake
6. Cutmill Pond
7. Valence Wood

☐ Estate Boundary
1771-1783
☐ Site of former mansion

Valence: A Landscape Transformed

Valence has a long-established history beginning in the mid-12th century when William, Earl of Gloucester gifted "ten parcels of undisturbed land at Brasted"[1] to Haimo de Valoines (or Valoniis) for his services to the Crown. The first recorded dwelling, probably a farmstead, was built towards the end of the 15th century by William Middleton,[2] and over the ensuing centuries the size of the estate and the number of dwellings grew, along with the fortunes of its various owners. By 1753, when the politician and naval commander Captain Peter Denis (1713-1788) took ownership, the estate had expanded to 215 hectares including gardens, orchards, woodland and farmland as well as farm buildings and a not insubstantial mansion, known as Valence House.[3] It is also clear that, by this time, a designed landscape featuring an abundance of water already existed at Valence, as it was described vividly by the travelling prelate and anthropologist, Dr Richard Pococke, on his visit in 1754. Pococke refers to a 'serpentine river' and 'canals' and, in particular, a view from the mansion of a spectacularly high water cascade flowing into the pond below.[4] The rocks over which the water once flowed are clearly evident today, as is the pond basin found some ten metres below, the form and structure of which pay testament to its early to mid-18th century origins.[5]

In 1771, ownership passed to a politician of some standing, the Earl of Hillsborough.[6] Hillsborough, no doubt taking advantage of the Enclosure Acts, acquired an additional farm and even more land than his predecessors. Valence now became known as Hill Park and Hill Park Farm. Over the next ten years, evidence suggests that Hillsborough, ably assisted by Lancelot 'Capability' Brown and his junior partner, the architect Henry Holland, gradually transformed the mansion and 263 hectares of the former Valence landscape. This transformation was certainly acknowledged by Hasted in his survey of the estate for the period between 1797 and 1801: he testifies to Hillsborough having "almost re-built this seat, and greatly improved the park and grounds about it".[7] The changes

55

to which Hasted refers, and the scale of Brown's involvement, become more apparent when documentary and cartographic evidence are examined.

Key evidence taken from Brown's personal accounts shows that, only one year after he bought the estate, Hillsborough commissioned Brown to make 'improvements' at Valence. A contractual agreement was set up between them, and a series of payments amounting to £1200 was made to Brown between 1772 and 1775. Although an annotation in his personal accounts, probably in Brown's hand, indicates that a debt of £50 remained outstanding,[8] the sum of £1200 was clearly substantial, converting to at least £140,000 today. Regrettably, but not untypically, Brown failed to record any further details. According to one Brown scholar, however, a similar amount (£1368) was paid to Brown during the 1760s by Sir William Codrington, at Dodington in Gloucestershire, for the building of 'lakes and fine contouring in a narrow Cotswold valley'.[9] The likelihood that Brown did similar work at Valence is supported by comparisons between the Andrews, Dury and Herbert map of 1769 (fig.1) and the estate map[10] and Ordnance Survey drawings of 1798-9 (figs.2 and 3).

The later maps show (coincidentally, in a narrow valley) a large

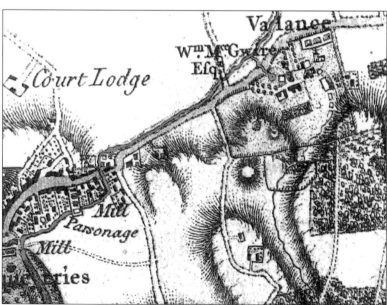

Figure 1.
Andrews, Dury and
Herbert map, 1769
Courtesy: Kent
History and Library
Centre

serpentine lake (at least 0.5 hectares), encompassing an island, where none existed before, together with some remodelling of the fishponds further north.

Importantly, the same evidence also reveals that, by 1798-9, other major changes had been made, adding to the transformation of the landscape from some thirty years earlier. The nature and the scale of these changes were distinctly characteristic of Brown's 'naturalistic' landscaping, and arguably, from evidence outside his accounts and other commissions, indicate a greater degree of involvement than the payments in his personal accounts would otherwise suggest. In this respect, one of Brown's biographers makes the particularly valid point:

> '...there are pitfalls in reading his accounts. He was working harder than these entries reveal, for Burghley, Petworth and Temple Newsam in Yorkshire (to name but three) were active at the time, but do not appear in the accounting window.'[11]

The earlier map of 1769 shows quite clearly that the Valence landscape was defined by formal avenues leading to and from the principal building, together with ponds and meandering streams, enveloped within steep-sided hills and dense woodland. A series of outbuildings and what appears to be a

Figure 2. (left) Estate map (Dyson, Lambarde and Larking) 1799
Courtesy: Kent History and Library Centre

Figure 3. (right) Ordnance Survey drawing 1798-9
Courtesy: British Library

church, or possibly a dovehouse[12] complete with its tower, lie towards the north-east with walled kitchen gardens immediately beyond. By stark contrast, the later maps of 1798-9 depict large areas of parkland studded with trees dominating the landscape. One avenue to the north-east has been removed and replaced with a driveway that divides to form a circuitous route around the north park before arriving with a grand sweep in front of the mansion. The second avenue, a lime avenue to the north-west, is shown to have remained, but has been extended, also with limes.[13] Clearly, the avenue was specifically contrived not only to define the east-west boundary, but also to provide another circuit around the park, and offer glimpses of the early to mid-18th century waterfall and pond that remained in situ. Individual trees are scattered around the parkland, and informal clumps appear to form a backdrop to the mansion to the south-west and the south-east. Towards the north-east, more open parkland appears where buildings once stood, and in Brown's true style, a perimeter serpentine belt of trees appears to obscure the kitchen gardens beyond. Dense woodland to the far south-east has been thinned to reveal merging pathways providing views and vistas and access to other areas of the park. In essence, it may be seen that all of these changes characterised the work of Brown,[14] and no doubt reflected the aspirations of Brown's patrons such as Hillsborough, as well as the cultural, social and political attitudes of the time.

It has long been recognised that Brown, along with some earlier, influential predecessors and patrons, such as the landscape architect William Kent, his patrons the Earl of Burlington and Viscount Cobham, shunned formality in favour of more naturalistic landscapes. Certainly during the relative peaceful years of the early-to-mid decades of the 18th century, the political landscape dominated by the Whigs heralded a more liberal constitution emanating towards greater enlightenment of ideas in certain social circles and cultural spheres of music, art and literature. Nowhere was this made more manifest symbolically, than in the sphere of landscape garden design, whereby the rigid formalism of late 17th to early 18th century gardens was almost completely swept away, and replaced with what was to become the phenomenon of the English Landscape Movement, whose chief protagonist was Brown.

At Valence, Brown's ingenuity to create a naturalistic landscape would have been tested, as it lies on the north slope of the Greensand Ridge, where the topography veers between undulating sloping ground, dense woodland and a steep-sided narrow valley which stretches downhill from south to north for one kilometre. Nevertheless, by the 1770s, Brown had gained a considerable reputation for skilful earth-moving and dam-building, which he almost certainly demonstrated with the building of the expansive, half-hectare serpentine lake known as Middle Lake (fig.4). The water came from a powerful natural spring via the 13th-century Cutmill Pond to the far south, which in turn fed the meandering stream flowing north. Cutmill Pond, however, is known to rest on dense Atherfield clay, whilst to the north, Middle Lake rests on particularly porous Hythe beds. These beds would have presented considerable problems with holding water unless the Atherfield clay had been introduced to line the lake. Notably, the existence of a 'dell'[15] situated to the south of Cutmill Pond, strongly suggests that clay would have been excavated from this far southern area of the estate before being transferred northwards to Middle Lake. It is also clear from the Ordnance Survey drawing (fig.3) that a large island[16] was built on the lake which may have served both aesthetic and practical

Figure 4.
Middle Lake looking north, showing boathouse, 1929
Courtesy: John Lochen

**Figure 5.
Middle Lake in
Summer 2015,
looking South**
*Courtesy: Jacs
Taylor-Smith*

purposes. Lochen puts forward the plausible explanation that
this large island 'may have been built to restrain water from
disappearing down a swallow hole'.[17] Problems with holding
water still persist today, in the 21st century, and have led to
some narrowing of the lake (fig.5). The Ordnance Survey
drawing also indicates a spur, or canal, that extends north-
eastwards from the lake, and possibly a weir at a point where
the spur joins the lake. A weir is clearly shown on the first
edition Ordnance Survey map of 1869, and demonstrates an
approach to water management by Brown that bears similarities
to work at Leeds Abbey and North Cray Place.

It is also likely that the level of the Hythe soil was reduced,
enabling the creation of more open, gently sloping ground and
the broad level path leading to the lake, which remain to this
day (fig.6). As Mayer argues, Brown was known generally
to have instructed his foremen to: 'Make the sides sloping
and keep the edges a neat Turf....Lay the Earth at the nearest
advantage making the adjacent Grounds slope gradually
to the edge of the Lake.'[18] Such feats of 18th-century

civil engineering were facilitated by the new earth-moving machinery ushered in by the Agricultural Revolution.

Although a major social, economic and cultural upheaval to rural life, the Agricultural Revolution was undoubtedly pivotal in helping to support Brown's ambitions and those of his patrons. The latter were keen to capitalise on their wealth-creating estates, and to acquire at the same time a landscape that was aesthetically pleasing. By the time of Brown's commission at Valence, the Enclosure Acts were already well established, allowing entitled landowners such as Hillsborough to seize common land as well as public rights of way, and where necessary remove whole villages. It is known that Brown was not averse to taking advantage of these opportunities for radical alteration, having removed the villages at Croome in Worcestershire, Stowe in Buckinghamshire and Houghton in Norfolk.[19] At Valence, there was no village within the estate to remove, but clearly, as the 1798-9 maps show, alterations were extensive with routes in and out of the estate diverted and buildings demolished, particularly to the north-east. Moreover, it may well be the case that Hillsborough (who was out of ministerial office during the years of the Brown commission) was referring to Valence when writing to his under-secretary, William Knox:

> 'I have totally forgotten that I was ever concerned in
> public business, and am so employed in church
> building, road making, farming and every rural
> occupation that belongs to an estate and a country

Figure 6.
Middle Lake in
Winter 2011, looking
South

gentleman that I go to bed every night very much tired, and find little time for anything else.'[20]

By the time of the Hillsborough commission, Brown had gained a considerable reputation as a landscape architect and was much in demand. But his commissions extended far beyond landscape works, and included the building of many country houses, garden buildings, bridges and even the occasional church. Few of these would have been executed, however, without the support of others, such as site engineers, builders and master craftsmen to name but a few. And it has long been established, by his biographer Dorothy Stroud in particular, that when in circa 1770 Brown took on as his business partner the young architect and future son-in-law, Henry Holland, it was to mark the beginning of a particularly important 'close collaboration' that was to continue until Brown's death in 1783.[21] It must be remembered that Brown was never a trained architect, and along with Stroud, Mayer has similarly argued that Brown would come to rely upon Holland, as he did with Holland's father before him, to carry out 'complex architectural commissions'.[22] Both the Stroud and Mayer statements are undoubtedly true, but evidence also suggests that Brown relied upon Holland earlier than was originally thought, at least from the outset of their partnership if not before.

Figures 7 and 8. Extracts from Henry Holland's price books, 1767-1772
Courtesy: Sir John Soane's Museum, London

Rare surviving evidence,[23] from two of Holland's three price

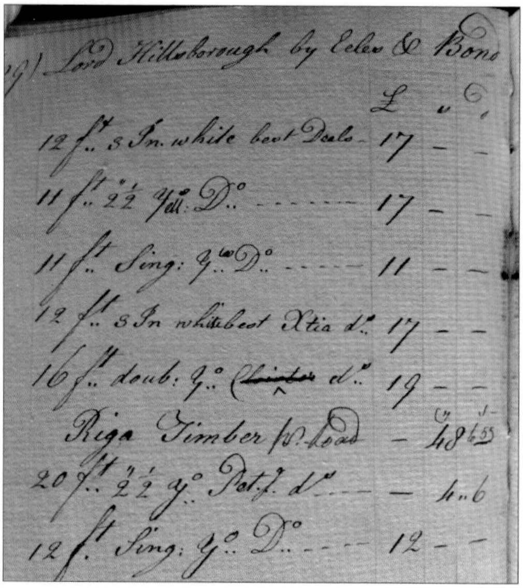
Lord Hillsborough by Eeles & Bond
12 ft.. 3 In. white best Deals .. 17 – –
11 ft.. 2½ Yell: Do. ...... 17 – –
11 ft. Sing: 4.. Do. ...... 11 – –
12 ft.. 3 In whitebest Xtia do. 17 – –
16 ft.. doub: 4.. do. 19 – –
Riga Timber pr. Load – 48 ..
20 ft.. 2½ 4o Petf. do. – 4..6
12 ft. Sing: 4o Do. ..... 12 – –

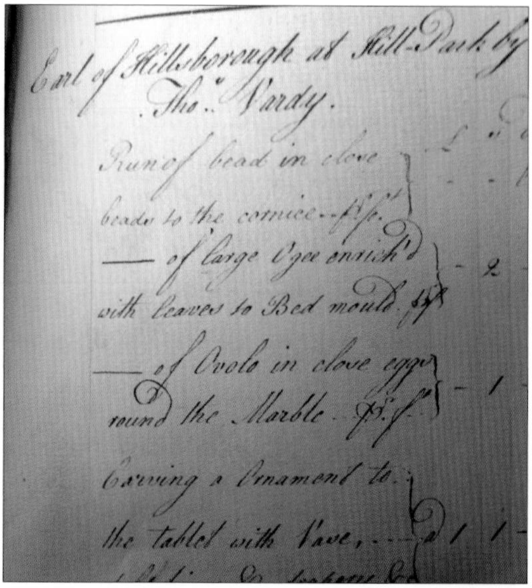
Earl of Hillsborough at Hill-Park by Tho.s Vardy.
Run of bead in close beads to the cornice .. ft.
— of large Ogee enrich'd with leaves to Bed mould ... 2
— of Ovolo in close egg round the Marble ... 1
Carving a Ornament to the tablet with Vase, ... 1 1

Figure 9.
Hill Park mansion,
showing cascade, J.P
Neale, circa 1819
*Courtesy: British
Library*

books dated between 1767 and 1772, shows that a number
of carvers, masons and builders were employed by Holland
himself to carry out various Brown commissions, including
internal and external refurbishments to the Valence mansion
(figs.7 and 8). Interior decoration at Valence included the
carving of cornices, friezes and chimney pieces (the latter,
embellished with dolphins and drapery, being the work of
the master carver, Thomas Vardy).[24] Holland also employed
builders to carry out bricklaying, tiling and roof repairs using
Welsh slate.[25] However, as Holland was very much the junior
partner at this stage of their collaboration, it is unlikely that
he would have taken responsibility for the mansion's major
refurbishments unless it was under Brown's overall direction.

There are further indications that design changes to the
mansion's facade were also undertaken at the same time.[26]
And despite assertions that Brown 'dispensed almost
completely with classical references to Arcadia',[27] Neale's
print of circa 1819 (fig.9) shows that the external architecture
of the Valence mansion followed a distinct, albeit restrained,
Palladian style of classical proportions, complete with portico,
supporting columns and pediment.[28] Moreover, the mansion's
facade bears marked similarities to the classical Palladianism of
Claremont in Surrey. Built by Brown for Lord Clive of India
between 1769 and 1773, it also coincided with the Valence

Figure 10.
Sketch of the lime
avenue and model
dairy, Louisa Baillie,
1842-4
Courtesy: John Lochen

commission. The Claremont commission was a particularly prestigious one for Brown, but once again, he demonstrated great faith in his junior partner, by delegating responsibility for Claremont's interior designs to Holland, just as Brown appeared to do at Valence.[29]

Evidence also strongly suggests that the Brown-Holland collaboration continued at Valence well into the 1770s. A further reference to 'Arcadia' was also apparent in the design of a model dairy, commissioned by the Earl of Hillsborough, for Lady Hillsborough, in 1777. The overall design, depicted in a mid-19th century sketch (fig.10) drawn by Louisa Baillie, the daughter of a later owner, shows the building situated at the eastern end of the lime avenue. Resembling a grand rotunda, complete with columnar arches and a domed roof, it would not have appeared out of place set amongst the garden temples at Stowe. Furthermore, Baillie's sketch of the dairy is particularly important when considering its architect, as it bears more than a passing resemblance to that found in Holland's sketchbook, together with details of the dairy's interior, in Holland's hand on the reverse page, and specifically inscribed, 'July 7th 1777, Lady Hillboro'. The dairy's interior,[30] was particularly grandiose and described in the sales particulars of 1857 as:

> '... expensively fitted with marble shelving, and a black and white marble floor, the walls covered with Dutch tiles.'[31]

As at Stowe, notions of grandeur and fashionable taste were perhaps the preserve of Brown's patrons, and in this instance particularly of Lady Hillsborough, rather than Brown himself; this being so, the Valence commission may also serve to demonstrate Brown's flexibility to accommodate the particular wishes of his patrons.

In 1783, Brown's death coincided with Hillsborough's sale of the entire 263 hectare Valence estate to John Cottin for the sum of £19,000. As with others before them, the sales particulars of 1783 are recorded in detail.[32] As well as the Valence mansion, farms and associated livestock, gardens, orchards, woodlands, watercourses, ponds and fish pools are all listed for sale. Also listed is 'the newly erected dairy' as well as 'a newly erected Gothic Temple' and in the kitchen gardens 'a newly erected greenhouse, a hothouse with hothouse plants' and a 'newly erected fruithouse therein'. Such evidence suggests that the building of the Gothic Temple and the kitchen garden buildings would have coincided with the building of the dairy from 1777 onwards (the latter already attributed to the Brown-Holland collaboration) and, therefore, were part of the same Brown commission. As there is no evidence that anyone other than Brown and his junior partner were involved with Valence during the Hillsborough years, it must surely follow that attribution for the late-18th century transformation ultimately rests with Brown.

In 1819, the draughtsman and author, J P Neale, recalled that the park itself was the:

> 'distinguishing beauty of this delightful residence...a winding valley...considerable hills, sometimes almost precipitous...at other times, a broad and level slope to the edge of the lake below, in some places studded with majestic oaks...a stream of pellucid water brawls along the bottom of the valley. ...the brook tumbles over a precipitous rock of natural production, the depth of 30 feet into a dark pool below....On the east and north are open sweeps which are gradually lost on the horizon or in the surrounding country.'[33]

Doubtless, Brown, who was not averse to retaining picturesque features within his landscapes,[34] would have warmed to such a description. The ensuing two centuries, however, would witness substantial changes to the landscape and the gradual fragmentation of Valence.

By the mid-19th century, the third Earl of Norbury, Hector John Toler, favoured the return of the then more fashionable formal principles of garden design. Expansive areas of parkland north and south of the mansion were altered to create formal parterres and geometric-shaped beds, whilst at the same time 'flower gardens and highly ornamental American shrubs and trees' were planted; 'a fine avenue of limes' was retained as was the 'magnificent cascade'; a fountain was created and gravel walks extended; more buildings sprang up, including a 'rustic' summer house, and a conservatory, cottages and stables designed by the architect Lewis Vuillamy (1791-1871)[35] all of which are recorded or illustrated in the sales particulars[36] and a detailed lithograph of 1857 (fig.11).

The farms, now under separate ownership, continued to be used for arable farming, sheep and cattle grazing. Hop growing was introduced, and more walled kitchen gardens and glasshouses were built to grow produce for the burgeoning market-gardening industry. A new mansion known as Dunsdale was also built to the far south-west, and the landscape architect Edward Milner (1819-1884) was commissioned by Dunsdale's new owner, Joseph Kitchen, to design the surrounding gardens and a new lake.

By the end of the 19th century, the refurbished Palladian-style mansion had been destroyed and, on the instructions of Valence's new owner, Norman Watney, was replaced with a new Victorian, Gothic-style mansion to the south-west. Henry Ernest Milner (1845-1906) was commissioned to design the garden surrounding the new mansion, and following in his father's footsteps, designed yet more formal parterres and re-modelled the fishponds south of the Middle Lake, to form Neptune Pond.[37]

Today, in the 21st century, notwithstanding numerous changes of ownership and the depletion of the parkland

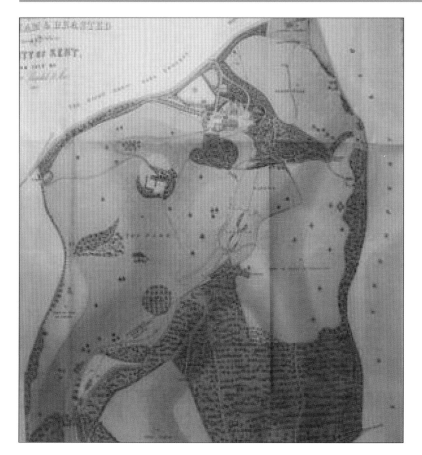

Figure 11.
Valence estate map,
1857
Courtesy: Kent History
and Library Centre

with the development of a golf course and new housing, the topographical nature of the landscape overall, with its undulating hills, steep sided valleys and woodland, is much the same as it was described by Neale in 1819. Elements of the 18th-century parkland are still discernible, as are the distinguishing boundary tree belts.

The once majestic lime avenue however, is now reduced to a small number of surviving trees, the kitchen garden is a housing estate, and Lady Hillsborough's dairy has long since disappeared. Nevertheless, the water, once so lyrically described by Neale, continues to flow from Cutmill Pond in the far south of the estate, to the newly restored Fountain Pond in the far north. More particularly, it is to be hoped that recent repairs and restoration of the serpentine lake, arguably Brown's focal point in the landscape, will ensure its survival for generations to come.

References

1   Lochen, p.14 The name Valence probably derives from Haimo de Valoines who took possession of the Brasted land in Kent between 1147 and 1148
2   Philipott
3   Kent History and Library Centre, R. A. Vestey, collection of title deeds, sales particulars, plans and maps 1579-1921, WU8 T/1
4   Pococke, pp.71-74
5   Physical evidence found during a site survey in 2011 conducted by Kent Gardens Trust, recorded and published in The Kent Compendium of Historic Parks and Gardens for Sevenoaks District, Valence and Dunsdale, Westerham, May 2012
6   Marshall, Wills Hills (1718-93) – Family Background and Political Beginnings. The first Marquess of Downshire was created Viscount Hillsborough in the Irish peerage in 1751. He was MP for Warwick from 1741 until becoming a member of the House of Lords from 1756. In 1772, he was elevated to the British peerage as the Earl of Hillsborough. He was regarded as ambitious and self-seeking and, though well-connected (Grenville, Fox and Halifax were friends), he was not generally well-regarded. He held several government posts including President of the Board of Trade and Secretary of State for the Colonies.
7   Hasted (1972 edition), vol.III, p.171
8   Royal Horticultural Society Lindley Libraries, The Account Book of Lancelot Brown, 1764-1788 (unpublished manuscript), p.85
9   Brown, p.160
10 Kent History and Library Centre, Dyson, Lambarde and Larking, Estate map 1799, WU8 T/1
11 Brown, p.163
12 Sales particulars from 1724 onwards (for example the Indenture of 26th February 1724 and the Bargain and Sale of 28th June 1753) verify the existence of dovehouses on the estate, but there are no references to a church. Kent History and Library Centre, Vestey papers, WU8 T/1
13 Site survey conducted in 2011 by Kent Gardens Trust showed that the lime avenue is partially extant.
14 Lennon, pp.239-240. The author refers to correspondence between Lord Bruce, Charles Bill, Mr. Winckles and Brown concerning Tottenham Park and Savernake Forest, Wiltshire from 1764 to the 1770s and observes that: 'The correspondence typically consists of queries for Brown, and his responses conveying details of the layout of features in the landscape around the house and forest. From this correspondence a number of tree planting features can be pinpointed to the period 1764-69. All of these without exception refer to serpentine rides, informal clumps and occasional plantations. Nowhere are there references to axial layouts, symmetrical platoons or straight avenues.'
15 Lochen, p.62
16 It is likely that a second, smaller island, clearly shown on the 1857 estate map, was built at the same time.
17 Lochen, p.62
18 Mayer, p.44
19 Ibid. p.37
20 Marshall, Wills Hills (1718-93) - Out of Office 1772-1779. On 27th April 1778,

Hillsborough was granted permission by three Justices of the Peace to divert a road adjoining his estate, known as Bavener's Lane. Hillsborough bought the road for £21 which was then blocked up as it was not wide enough to travel on, and another road was built immediately beyond the southern boundary of the Hill Park (Valence) estate. Kent History and Library Centre, Q/RH2/6

21   Stroud, 'Capability Brown' (1975 edition) p.144

22   Mayer, p.35

23   Stroud, op.cit p.176. All of Holland's office papers were destroyed after his death by his nephew, Henry Rowles.

24   White. Thomas Vardy was a carver from Grosvenor Square and the brother of John Vardy (1717/18-1765), an English architect and close associate of William Kent.

25   Henry Holland's 'Price Books', Soane archives, case 128, Sir John Soane's Museum, London

26   Ibid. case 129

27   Mayer, p.30

28   J.P.Neale's drawing reproduced in The Kent Compendium of Historic Parks and Gardens for Sevenoaks District, Valence and Dunsdale, Westerham, May 2012

29   It is notable that Holland was engaged on the interiors of Claremont between 1771 and 1772, at the same time as the Valence commission. Holland was also engaged on the interior of Leeds Abbey and appointed Henry Wood to carry out the carving, as he did at Claremont. Holland's Price Books, Soane archives, case 128; Jenkins pp.733-4; and Stroud, p.143

30   Henry Holland's 'Miscellaneous Sketches', 1777, SM Volume 38, Sir John Soane's Museum, London. It appears from Holland's annotated pencil drawings specifically inscribed 'July 7th 1777 Dairy Lady Hillboro', that Holland may also have executed his own designs for the interior of Lady Hillsborough's dairy. A drawing, not signed, depicting a rotunda appears on the reverse page.

31   Kent History and Library Centre, freehold estate particulars of The Sale by Auction by Messrs. Beadel and Sons, London on Tuesday, 7th July 1857, WU8 EII

32   Kent History and Library Centre, Sales Particulars between the Earl of Hillsborough and John Cottin, 28th May 1783, WU8 T/1

33   Neale

34   Kent History and Library Centre, R.A. Vestey papers, WU8 T/1. The sales particulars of 1766 includes a description of the cascade with a statue of Neptune at the head of the cascade and boats on the pond. The cascade and the pond were features that were retained.

35   Vuillamy, p.142

36   Kent History and Library Centre, Sales Particulars, 7th July 1857, WU8/E11

37   See the chronology of historic development in The Kent Compendium report on Valence.

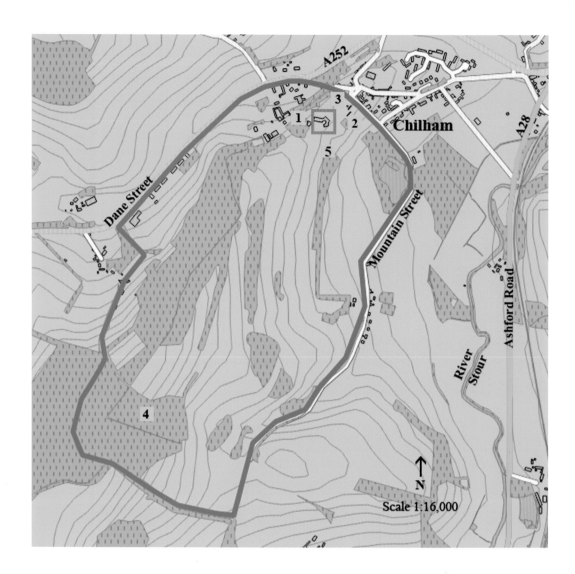

Chilham Castle in today's setting

Key features

1. Medieval keep
2. Walled garden
3. Main entrance
4. Felborough Wood
5. 17th century avenue

☐ Boundary of designed landscape 1779-81
☐ Chilham Castle

Figure 1. Chilham Castle The Seat of Thomas Heron Esq. by Rev. Samuel Rastall 1777
Courtesy: Kent History and Library Centre

Chilham Castle: A Fine Landscape Improved

A view of Chilham Castle drawn by the Reverend Samuel Rastall in 1777 (fig.1) shows the grounds of the Castle as Lancelot 'Capability' Brown would have seen them when he first visited in late July 1777.[1] The view is taken from Julaber's Grave (fig.2), south-east of the Castle, a famous and historic landmark and a favoured point chosen by artists to paint views of the Castle.[2]

This view, which was included in Edward Hasted's account of Chilham Castle,[3] shows the 17th century mansion known as Chilham Castle standing on an eminence close to the remains of a Norman keep with four terraces immediately in front on

71

the falling ground below. A wall marks the south-east and south-west boundaries of the formal gardens which is pierced by a section of railings to form a claire-voie. The gardens are surrounded by parkland richly planted with groups of trees. A substantial group of trees has been planted to the south-east of the Castle (far left in the drawing) providing a frame for the prospect of Julaber's Grave. A belt of trees can be seen on the north-west horizon. To complete the picture, some deer are running within the outer boundary wall.

Chilham Castle was well known for its fine views and was praised by John Harris[4] in his History of Kent and by William Gilpin.[5] Edward Hasted was likewise enthusiastic in The History and Topographical Survey of the County of Kent:

> 'The parish of Chilham is situated exceedingly pleasant, in a fine healthy part of the county, ...the river Stour runs along the eastern part of the parish...., and on the height above it the noted mount of earth, usually called Juliberrie's grave. On an eminence, almost adjoining to the opposite or west side of the road is the village ... and the antient castle, with the stately mansion and park of Chilham. On the opposite side from which there is a most beautiful view over the spacious Ashford vale, through which the river Stour directs its course .... all together forming a most rich and luxuriant prospect.'[6]

The view to the east of the Castle was also a fine one, affording a glimpse of Canterbury Cathedral as is shown in the

Figure 2. Prospect of Julaber's Grave from Chilham, by W. Stukeley, 1724
Courtesy: Mr and Mrs S. Wheeler

72

illustration of Chilham by William Watts (fig.3) in his Seats of the Nobility where he says *'It is a spacious, stately mansion, finely situated for the Command of several beautiful Prospects, particularly of a Valley below it, which is watered by the River Stour.'*[7]

Figure 3. The Seat of Thomas Heron Esquire, by William Watts, 1779
Courtesy: Kent History and Library Centre

Chilham Castle has a long history. After the Norman Conquest the prosperous manor of Chilham, which was described in the Domesday Book as having 6 mills, was held by King William's half-brother, Bishop Odo. The Normans built a keep on the hill overlooking the river Stour and Julaber's grave. In 1612 the manor was acquired by Dudley Digges (1583-1639), an ambitious and able politician, a diplomat and entrepreneur, and an investor in the Virginia Company of London. Knighted by James I in 1607, he became Master of the Rolls in 1638.

Digges replaced an earlier manor house[8] with a magnificent red brick mansion immediately adjacent to the keep, taking advantage of the extensive views to the south and east over the Stour valley and Julaber's Grave. Digges, the son of a noted mathematician, had the Castle built in the shape of a hexagon with the south side left open. Digges was ambassador to Muscovy (The Grand Duchy or Principality of Moscow) from 1618-19 and took as one of his entourage the celebrated naturalist and gardener John Tradescant the Elder (1570–1638) who brought back several new plants from the expedition. Tradescant worked for Edward, Lord Wotton in Canterbury between 1615 and 1623 and it seems very likely that he had a hand in the design of the garden at Chilham which Digges laid out to complement his new house. John Harris describes the gardens in 1719: *'The Prospect is very fine and the gardens laid out in a Terras-manner, one under another, in good order, and rendered yet more ornamental by a fine Wilderness work of Hornbeam'.*[9] The Wilderness can be seen on later maps (figs.5 and 6) laid out on the east side of the Castle in an area which is still planted with trees and now known as the Quiet Garden.

Rastall's view of the Castle (fig.1), some 150 years after it was built, shows the slope on the south-east side of the new house carved into about four parallel terraces stepping down the steep slope to the south-east and retained by vertical walls, the whole edifice providing a magnificent setting for the house in its elevated position. The terraces, which are typical of grand Tudor gardens, still form the main elements of the garden today though they have been altered and extended by subsequent owners. The lowest terrace is said[10] to have been used as a bowling green from about 1630 which would have been typical for that period. The terraces are shown with plants, perhaps fruit trees, trained against the retaining walls.

Sir Dudley Digges is reputed to have enclosed about 25 acres of parkland south-west of his new mansion,[11] thus setting in train the development of the park which so impressed Brown many years later. Some ancient sweet chestnut trees still survive to the south-west of the terraces which may be the remnants of a 17th century avenue.[12]

After Digges' death in 1639 the estate remained in his family until 1724 when it was sold to James Colebrooke (1681–1752) a wealthy banker. Colebrooke appears to have quickly embarked on a programme of extending and embellishing Digges' park. In 1728[13] he was able to enclose 23 acres immediately beyond the terraces (which became known as the

Figure 4. View of Chilham Keep, Castle and Gardens, by Samuel & Nathaniel Buck, 1741
Courtesy: National Trust/Charles Thomas

Paddock[14]) by diverting the road which ran around the south-east boundary of the Castle grounds.[15] More land to the south and west was enclosed in 1733, bringing the total acreage of the park to about 300.[16]

An engraving dated 1741 by Samuel and Nathaniel Buck (fig.4) shows the Castle and its grounds after these additions. The Paddock is an expanse of grass planted with occasional trees and bounded by a wall along the recently diverted road which now forms the south-east boundary. Beyond the road a double avenue runs south-east to the banks of the River Stour, possibly axial on the open front of the house. The 'claire-voie', which is shown in fig.1 allowed views of the Castle from the road and from the Castle along the avenue to the river beyond. West of the Castle the old field boundaries remain. The Buck engraving depicts a substantial number of trees close to the north-east front of the Castle which may represent the triple avenue which lined the main approach to its front entrance from Chilham village and the Wilderness. Both these features are recorded on the Andrews, Dury and Herbert map of 1769 (fig.5). In the right foreground, some water-filled channels or leats are

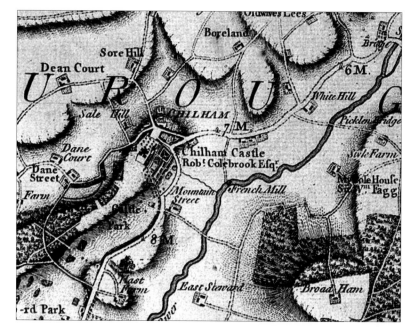

Fig. 5. Andrews, Dury and Herbert, A Topographical Map of the County of Kent (London, 1769)
Courtesy: Kent Library and History Centre

depicted on the low-lying land close to the river Stour which could perhaps be a system for managing it as a water meadow.

James Colebrooke, or more probably his son Robert (1718–1784), who came into possession of the estate on his father's death in 1752, was responsible for introducing a more naturalistic style of landscaping to the park. By 1769, the double avenue framing the view to the south-east through the 'claire-voie' seems to have been felled as it is not shown on Andrews, Dury and Herbert's map of that date (fig.5); intersecting rides through Felborough Wood south-west of the house, typical of the irregularity of the new style that designers and garden writers such as Stephen Switzer (1682-1745) were proposing, can also be seen on the map together with several clumps of trees. These, typical of the improvements made to parks in the mid-18th century may have been created by the removal of hedges with just a few of the best trees retained. Substantial blocks of trees are shown along Dane street, the north-west boundary of the park, another common feature of 18th century parks.

Brown was, by the 1760s, the most influential exponent of this type of landscape design, having developed the early naturalistic style inspired by Sir John Vanbrugh (1664-1726), Stephen Switzer and finally William Kent to its highest point. There is no evidence that Brown was employed by Robert Colebrooke but it seems likely that the changes made to the park in the 1760s were at least influenced by Brown's work, which Robert is likely to have seen at first hand. His brother Sir George Colebrooke (1729-1809) had inherited Gatton Hall in Surrey from his elder brother James in 1761, and payments in Brown's account book are evidence of the substantial work of creating a lake and plantations[17] he undertook for Sir George from 1762 to 1768.

Another possible connection with Brown is that Robert Colebrooke (who seems to have been a lavish spender) employed the leading architect of the time, Sir Robert Taylor, to build a grandiose family mausoleum (demolished in the 19th century) in St Mary's church in Chilham. Brown worked at several sites where Sir Robert Taylor was employed as architect, for example Mount Clare in Roehampton and Heavening Hall in Suffolk.[18]

The enhancement of the romantic setting of the keep, especially seen from the favoured view from Julaber's grave across the Stour, seems to have been another example of Robert Colebrooke's efforts to naturalise Chilham's landscape. Both the Watts and Rastall engravings (figs.1 and 3) show the ancient keep rising out of a dense tangle of trees and shrubs and with vegetation sprouting from its ruinous walls, much changed from its stark appearance in Buck's view of 1741 (fig.4). Brown would surely have approved as he is known to have embellished ruins in a similar way, for example at Warwick Castle and Battle Abbey. The planting around the keep can be seen on the Ordnance Survey drawing of 1789[19] (fig.6) and in a view of 1800 (fig.7) of the mansion and keep.

Robert Colebrooke's extravagance[20] led to increasing debts[21] and eventually his trustees were forced to sell Chilham in 1774. The purchaser, Thomas Heron (1727-1794), was a wealthy lawyer from Newark-upon-Trent who embarked on a programme of repairs to the house and improvement and expansion of the estate, which he discussed in detail in letters to his brother, Sir Richard Heron, who was stationed in Dublin as Chief Secretary to the Lord Lieutenant in Ireland. This correspondence has fortunately survived and provides a remarkable insight into the changes he made to the park and gardens and his relationship with Brown.[22]

One of Heron's first actions was to fell the avenue of limes along the Castle's main, north-east approach from Chilham village and other trees on the estate. He made a new public road on the south-west side of the park, thereby adding 42 acres, including Felborough Wood, to the park. On 27th June 1777, he wrote to his brother: *'My new road and removal of the Park fence was completed yesterday. The Public have gained a more commodious and pleasant road. I have acqu'd gro'd where I was much straitned. The Park is exceedingly improved in Beauty on the side enlarged. Felbro' wood is also laid to the Park which is a great addition'.* Chilham's steward, Christopher Greaves (1742-1802), also seems to have been closely involved in the improvements to the estate. Heron told his brother that *'he is very useful and indeed necessary to*

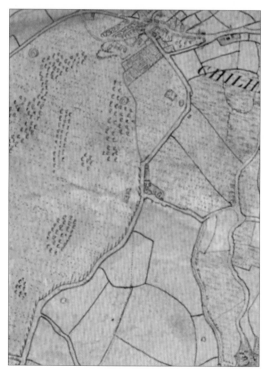

Figure 6.
Ordnance Survey
drawing 1789
Courtesy: British
Library

me; for I am so taken up in a variety of employments and have everything to form from chaos, that I should have a loss of him. I can depend on his Integrity attention and assiduity'. Greaves was a successful estate manager who also had sound knowledge of architectural practice, accountancy and finance. He wrote 'Antiquities of Chilham' in 1791[23] with Heron which gives an account of its history, much of which was passed on to Edward Hasted who was writing his book on the history of Kent at the time.[24]

In 1777, three years after buying Chilham, Thomas Heron decided to ask Brown to advise him on improvements to the park and gardens. Heron's regular correspondence with his brother gives a remarkably detailed account of the discussions which took place between him and Brown over the latter's proposals and the changes which were made to these as a result of Heron's active involvement (and possibly limited funds). They are, however, tantalisingly vague about how many of Brown's ideas were actually put into effect.

Brown seems to have been rather reluctant to come to Kent. In a letter to his brother written on 27th June 1777, Heron said that he had *'heard nothing from Brown. Greaves says he don't desire to see him for he will take a great deal of money and that we can do very well without him. I wish to see him, tho' I give him up. Greaves has been very attentive and judicious in the improvement'*.

Eventually Brown arrived at Chilham on 28th July 1777 and stayed for two days. His account book[25] states that he drew up a 'General Plan for the alterations to the Place'. Unfortunately this plan has not survived. Brown was clearly impressed with the landscape which had evolved over the previous 150 years and which is illustrated in the engraving by Samuel Rastall (fig.1). After the visit Thomas Heron reported to his brother on 1st August that Brown *'admires the situation and beauty of the grounds'* and had advised that *'there is little to do in the Park; it is so well wooded that it only wants a little opening.'* He did not recommend any new plantations but suggested *'some management of the Woods and Tillage of the Ground which will expel the Deer, to save an unreasonable expense of fencing against them.'* The deer were duly sold to a neighbour a few months later. Brown did not specify where the openings in the park should be, leaving Heron to decide these. *'He said there was little necessary; merely to follow fancy; the truth is he had no time for it'.* Perhaps Brown was uninterested in making small alterations to a landscape which was already close to his ideal.

Brown did, however, have definite views on improving the distant views of the Castle which were spoiled by the clutter of buildings, stables, farmyard and wood-yard around its main entrance from the village. In the same letter Heron reported that Brown *'says no building should appear with the Castle and he thinks the valey (sic) on that side very fine, and that the view of it from the Park should not be intercepted.'* There was much discussion over the next three years about a new site for the stables and farmyard. In January 1778, Brown produced a general plan for new stables and a coach house which Heron forwarded to his brother for his opinion on 16th January. Heron also sent alternative plans for stables and farmyard, prepared by Greaves, which he seemed to prefer. Regrettably, none of these plans has survived. Brown's preferred site for both stables and farmyard seems to have been on the north side of the Castle but they are not shown there until recorded on the Ordnance Survey edition of 1872, so it seems likely that, as Heron died in 1794, the works were implemented later.

Brown also seems to have thought that land to the south-east of the Castle between Mountain Street and the river Stour could be improved. Heron told his brother on 1st August 1777: *'The River he would enlarge and lay the earth on the low parts of the meadows, and drain them'.* It is unclear whether these proposals were carried out. Heron informed his brother on 26th October 1778 that *'The alteration of the Gardens, River, Plantations etc being matters of fancy may remain for more convenient times ...'.* The river does not seem to have been enlarged and its course appears to have remained more or less constant from that shown in the Andrews, Dury and Herbert map of 1769. However, the Buck view of Chilham in 1741 (fig.4) shows a network of ditches and water-filled channels on the low-lying land beside the River Stour which may be evidence of water meadow management. Water meadows were much admired in the 18th century both as agriculturally beneficial and aesthetically pleasing. Brown frequently included them in his designs for parkland[26] and it is possible that his proposals for Chilham included restoring or extending an existing system. There is evidence of water meadows at Chilham today: a grid of leats still exists in the area between Mountain Street and the river.[27] If indeed any of Brown's proposals for alterations to the water at Chilham were undertaken, it seems, in the light of the details in the Buck view, more likely that an existing system was restored rather than a new one established.

Brown is well-known for removing the formal gardens and parterres which had been fashionable in the 17th and early 18th centuries, substituting a sweep of grass right up to the walls of the house and eliminating the clear divide between the garden and the wider landscape. His first proposal for the gardens at Chilham in August 1777 was a rather limited scheme: *'to lay down that part of the garden before the House, except the upper terrases, which he considers a set-off to it.'* He clearly appreciated the dramatic setting of the house above the river Stour. On his second visit, in 1778, Brown appears to have modified his earlier plans. Heron reported to his brother on 26th August that the proposal now was that:

> *'All the gardens below the House [should be] destroyed and made a pasture open to the Paddock or otherwise used as most agreeable, and left at liberty for an approach. The wall of the upper Terras to be taken down and the ground from the House sloped to the wall of the Terras, to correspond with the slope before the house, the next Terras to remain entire, and the Wall which divides it from the Bowling Green to be the fence or boundary…'.*

An engraving by Watts published in 1779 (fig.3) shows the top terrace as it looked before the regrading required to make the angle of the slope *'correspond with the slope before the house'.* Brown's revised proposal involved simplifying the ground immediately around the house including removing the topmost of the 17th century terraces but retaining the lower terraces on the south-east side of the house in order to enhance its dramatic setting.

This work was soon put into effect. Heron reported on 26 October 1778 that *'The Levelling abt the House goes on very well, and I hope it will soon be done'*.

A view of the Castle by William Green in about 1800 (fig.7) illustrates the change to the landscape immediately around the Castle with the ground sloping gently away, an echo of the distant hills. As part of the adjustment of the levels the 'sunk fence and wall' (i.e. the ha-ha) was to be extended from the south-west corner of the lowest terrace, known as the Bowling Green, up to *'the clump on the mount near the Castle'*. The ha-ha, built of brick, is still in place allowing an uninterrupted view from the garden south-west over the park.

The alteration of the landscape around the Castle extended to its main approach from Chilham village. Heron had begun to re-fashion the area on the entrance front, before Brown arrived in 1777, by felling the avenue of limes which lined the short approach drive between the entrance gates standing on the west side of Chilham village square and the Castle's north-east front. The approach was given a radical redesign in which what had probably been Digges' short avenue was replaced by a generous forecourt with a carriage drive encircling a grass plat, representing a further relaxing of formality. The new layout was in place by 1789 as recorded on the Ordnance Survey

**Figure 7.
Chilham Castle the Seat of James Wildman Esq., by William Green published in Coloured Views of Kentish Seats of the Nobility and Gentry, George Wood, c1800**
Courtesy: Kent History and Library Centre

drawing of that date (fig.6). An engraving of a drawing by J.P. Neale published in 1825 (fig.8) shows the forecourt nearly fifty years later with an open expanse of grass in front of the Castle, embellished picturesquely with peacocks, much as Brown had designed it although the line of the carriage sweep has been altered.

Figure 8. (left) J.P. Neale Chilham Castle, Kent *Courtesy: Kent History and Library Centre*

Brown had made various proposals to improve the main entrance. His first suggestion, in 1777, was that the stables should be moved close to the entrance and that there should be *'a good gateway in the centre'* to shut out the village and a porter's lodge but Heron thought that the proximity of the village would mean that *'the gate or stables must be the constant lounge of the idle'* which a porter would be unable to control. Brown's detailed designs were received in January 1778 and it seems that he had heeded Heron's concerns and now proposed to move the site of the stables and farmyard, to the west side of the keep, where they are situated today, well out of sight of the Castle.

Once the decision had been reached to re-site the farmyard and create a new entrance and approach, Brown could design a suitably imposing gateway. This he did in January 1781 when he submitted plans for a lodge and gates.[28]   These, designed in the Gothic style, were shown in a later watercolour (fig.9) painted between 1850 and 1860 by Emily Wildman (1831-1906) daughter of James Beckford Wildman (1778–1867) who inherited the estate in 1816. The design with its crenellations, though on a smaller scale, has affinities with Brown's designs for Cardiff Castle and the Gothic lodge at Wardour Castle.

The discussions over the siting of the stables and farmyard show how readily Brown was willing to adapt his ideas to his clients' wishes without losing sight of his original aim, which in this case was to clear the immediate environs of the Castle allowing it to be viewed alone in imposing grandeur. He visited Chilham twice, in July 1777 and again in August 1778, after producing detailed designs in the January of that year which Heron travelled to Hampton Court to discuss with him in March 1778. On Brown's second visit to Chilham he *'made some variations in his plan'* and in December 1778 Heron wanted to remind Brown of *'the plans he is to draw for me'*. The extensive correspondence between Heron and his brother details the collaborative process between Brown and his patron. Brown seems to have been similarly flexible in his designs for a kitchen garden. Heron was very interested in the produce of his kitchen garden, the site of which seems to have been north-east of the Castle and bordering Mountain Street on its east side.

Figure 9.
Watercolour of the entrance to Chilham Castle by Emily Wildman c.1860
Courtesy: Mr. and Mrs. S. Wheeler

The Andrews, Dury and Herbert map of 1769 (fig.5) shows an enclosure here with diagonal paths, which is likely to have been the vegetable garden. Its location was conveniently situated close to the stables so that dung was easily accessible. There are frequent references in Heron's correspondence to fruit: for example in March 1777 he ordered Warrington red Gooseberry Plants and he grew melons, brocoli (sic) and asparagus as well as several varieties of Apples.[29]

Brown's first suggestion in July 1777 was for the new kitchen garden to be situated on the site of a Nursery *'and have a small addition at the bottom from the Paddock; this situation for the garden is from necessity; there being no other in any degree conven't'*. After Brown had made his second visit in August 1778, Heron reported on 26th August: *'Mr Brown was here last week. He has made some variations in his plan, which consist from a change in place for the Kitchen Garden.'* The new site was north-west of the Castle alongside Dane Street, close to the proposed new position for the stables. Heron continued: *'The Garden to be oblong having its sides to that road and the castle in order to open it as much as possible to the sun.'* Neither plan - for the garden or the stables - was implemented. However, a site for the kitchen garden was eventually settled on, close to the main entrance, where it remains today. Work on its construction was underway in 1779 as Heron wrote on 4th February: *'The Hot House must be a future consideration when the garden is done'*. By March, Brown had proposed a further feature as Heron wrote: *'Mr Brown has sent a drawing for a Green House which is very pretty & well designed'*. This would have been the centrepiece of the garden and was probably located on the north-west wall in which remnants of a heating system can be seen.[30] The kitchen garden is recorded on the Ordnance Survey drawing of 1789 (fig.6). Brown may also have designed a gardener's house in the south-east corner of the Kitchen Garden adjoining Mountain Street which later became known as the Elephant House.[31]

The sum of £412.10.0 was paid by Heron into Brown's account with Drummonds Bank on 2nd February 1781[32]. This is a relatively small sum compared to the £2,656 it cost Sir George Colebrooke for the landscaping at Gatton, or the £1,200 paid by

Figure 10. Chilham Castle Kent General View by J.P. Neale 1825
Courtesy: Kent History and Library Centre

the Earl of Hillsborough at Hill Park, and reflects the fact that the work which Brown undertook at Chilham was quite limited. His achievement there was to recognize the quality of the park, with its fine landscape potential already well developed, and to reassure his patron that little was needed to improve it, even leaving the remnants of the 17th century south avenue untouched (see fig.6).

Brown's designs for Chilham's landscape were implemented over a period of time and by different owners. Thomas Heron undertook perhaps the major part, levelling the top terrace, regrading the slope close to the Castle, and refashioning the main entrance in an informal style. The plans for new stables and farmyard were not put into effect until after 1789 but the kitchen garden and its hot house do seem to have followed Brown's plan, although the actual building operations may have been overseen by Heron's steward Christopher Greaves. The lake with its bridge, which is often attributed to Brown,[33] was the work of a later owner, Charles Stewart Hardy in 1869.[34]

86

Brown may have carried out some remedial work on the water meadows but there is no clear evidence for this.

The top terrace, removed by Brown, was reinstated and extended in the 19th century, probably by Charles Hardy when he employed David Brandon in 1861 to reconfigure the house. Charles Hardy was also responsible for demolishing Brown's entrance lodge and gates.[35]

Brown demonstrated his genius at Chilham largely through what he did not do. At the height of his career and fame, he did not consider it necessary to suggest more than modest changes to what was already a well-composed landscape. He recognised the nobility of Chilham's situation with its views, history and dramatic position and his proposals were designed to emphasise the grandeur of the Jacobean building standing proud on its eminence above the river Stour. That he was successful in this endeavour can be seen in the 1825 view of the Castle and the ancient keep nearby by J.P. Neale (fig.10). Brown has been criticised for sweeping away the topmost 17th century terrace and the formal gardens around the house; but these changes should be seen as part of his scheme to enhance the principal building and to harmonise its immediate setting, and the ancient keep, with the surrounding landscape, as is perhaps best illustrated in William Green's view of 1800 (fig.7). The removal of the buildings clustered around the Castle was proposed with the same overarching intention, as was the design of the simple and expansive entrance court shown in the engraving of J.P. Neale's 1825 drawing (fig.8). Although Brown was not commissioned to create a new landscape at Chilham, what he achieved there is a testament to his unerring eye for the harmonious quality of the landscape.

References
1   Lincolnshire Archive Office, Letter from Thomas Heron to his brother Richard Heron 1st August 1777, Stubton VII/E/1 (3 volumes)
2   Julaber's (there are various spellings) Grave is a Neolithic long barrow and is to this day a dramatic eye-catcher in the view from the Castle. In the 18th century it was thought to be the grave either of a giant called Julaber or of Quintus Laberius Durus, one of Julius Caesar's tribunes killed in battle with the Britons, and was itself a popular scene for artists.
3   Hasted, first edition, vol. III, pp.130-131
4   Harris, History of Kent
5   Gilpin, vol.II, p.129
6   Hasted (1972 edition), vol.VII, p.263
7   Watts, Plate LXXII
8   Hasted (1972 edition), vol.VII, pp. 274-5
9   Harris, op. cit.
10 Clapham, A. W. An Early Hall at Chilham Castle, Kent, The Antiquaries Journal, July 1928, (vol. VIII, No.3) pp. 349-353 (an account of excavations carried out by the author and Mortimer Wheeler)
11 Chilham Castle private archive, Antiquities of Chilham, collected by Thomas Heron Esq., 1791 and brought up to date by Charles Hardy, 1912 p.71
12 Chilham Castle private archive, Historic Landscape Survey and Restoration Proposals, Debois Landscape Survey Group, 2003, p.12
13 Kent History and Library Centre, Writ of Quod ad Damnum, 1728
14 Antiquities of Chilham p.71
15 Ibid.
16 Ibid.
17 Royal Horticultural Society, Lindley Library, The Account book of Lancelot 'Capability' Brown, 1764-1788 (unpublished manuscript), p.136
18 Original survey by George Pink, 1789, finished in 1801, British Library, OSD sheet 109-111, part 1, 3" to 1 mile
19 Ibid.
20 Seymour, vol. IV, p.249
21 and see Letter from Thomas Heron to his brother 17 May 1778 in which he says that Colebrooke was not able to pay £5 or £6 for repairs to their family Mausoleum (see note 22 below)
22 Lincolnshire Archive Office, Letters from Thomas Heron to his brother Richard Heron (1726-1805), Stubton VII/E/1. All the quotations from Heron's letters to his brother in this chapter are taken from this archive.
23 Chilham Castle private archive
24 Jessup, vol.56, pp.11-18
25 Royal Horticultural Society, Lindley Library, The Account book of Lancelot 'Capability' Brown, 1764-1788 (unpublished manuscript), p.9
26 See Historic England, Introduction to Heritage Assets: Water Meadows, p.8
27 Chilham Castle private archive, Historic Landscape Survey and Restoration Proposals, Debois Landscape Survey Group, 2003, p.20
28 Royal Horticultural Society, Lindley Library, The Account book of Lancelot 'Capability' Brown, 1764-1788 (unpublished manuscript), p.136
29 'I sent to the Hay on Friday an Hamper with apples, the Upper Division was in two

parts, Nonpareils & Aromatic Perfects, the next Lemon Pippins, at the Bottom Perfects for Cookery', Letter to Richard Heron, 10 Jan 1779

30 Chilham Castle private archive, Historic Landscape Survey and Restoration Proposals, Debois Landscape Survey Group, 2003, p.22

31 The listed building designation (Listing NGR TR0690853468) states that the building is late 18th century. It was at one time thought to have housed elephants but there is no evidence for this. The name may have arisen because of the dressed stone arches which ornament the front, would have been large enough for an elephant. (Chilham Castle private archive, Historic Landscape Survey and Restoration Proposals, Debois Landscape Survey Group, 2003 p.30)

32 Brown's accounts with Drummonds Bank now held by the Royal Bank of Scotland

33 Stroud, Capability Brown, 1st edition 1950, p.173. The reference is omitted from the revised edition 1975. Also the original listed building designation for the bridge over the lake (Listing NGR TR0694453315) describes it as being 18th century and 'Part of Capability Brown's landscaping'.

34 Chilham Castle private archive, Historic Landscape Survey and Restoration Proposals, Debois Landscape Survey Group, 2003, p.26

35 Ibid.

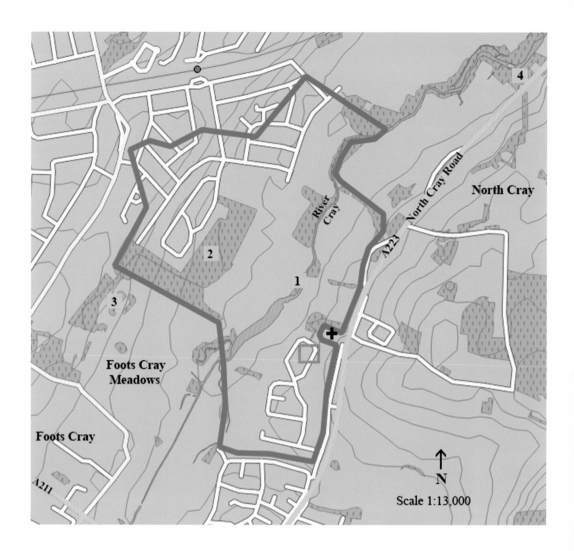

North Cray Place in today's setting

Key features

1. Five Arch Bridge
2. North Cray Wood
3. Site of former
   Foots Cray Place
4. Vale Mascal

☐ Boundary of designed
landscape in early 1780s

☐ Site of former
North Cray Place mansion

✚ St. James's Church

North Cray Place:
and Brown's Influence on Nearby Estates

The landscape and ownership history of North Cray Place and Foots Cray Place, which together now form Bexley's largest public open space, Foots Cray Meadows, are closely intertwined. Lying side by side on either side of the River Cray, which flows north into the Thames just north of Dartford, both estates share an origin in Neolithic and Roman settlements and are recorded as manors in the Domesday survey, circa 1086. North Cray was gifted from William the Conqueror to his half-brother Odo, Bishop of Bayeux; Foots Cray was in separate ownership, its name appearing to derive from a local landowner, Godwin Fot.[1]

Both estates already had a significant house and extensive formal gardens by the early 18th century which were transformed in the mid-to-late 18th century into new, naturalistic 'Arcadian' landscapes designed to evoke the classical idea of perfection formed by sweeping lawns, water and carefully placed groups of trees to create vistas. Although Foots Cray was the first, in the 1750s and 60s, to undergo this change, only North Cray could boast a landscape designed by the 18th-century's foremost landscape designer, Lancelot 'Capability' Brown. Thomas Coventry (1713-1797), who inherited the estate in 1778, was well-connected to say the least. His cousin was George William Coventry, the 6th Earl of Coventry (1722-1809), and it was he who commissioned for his estate at Croome what was to be Brown's first independent design of any scale (he worked on the site from 1747 to 1782) and it is arguably his finest surviving landscape. The North Cray commission came towards the end of this period, in c.1780, and this chapter seeks to explore the extent of Brown's involvement at North Cray Place and the possible influences on Coventry's aspirations to transform his estate. These influences include the transformation of two other nearby estates, Danson and Vale Mascal (not designed by Brown but which drew on his reputation to solve issues and propose improvements).

Remaining separately owned and landscaped until 1833, the two sites were united when the trustees of the marriage settlement of Thomas Coventry's godson sold North Cray to Lord Bexley,[2] Nicholas Vansittart (1766-1851). Divided again in the 1930s through the separate sale of North Cray, they were finally re-united in the 1950s and 60s by the provident purchase of the parkland of both estates by the local authority and re-named Foots Cray Meadows.[3] Such proactive purchase in the 20th century of former private estate land for a public open space probably secured the survival of Brown's landscape at North Cray, albeit now altered by neglect. Foots Cray's parkland benefitted similarly, as did that of nearby Danson Park, probably designed by Nathaniel Richmond (1724-1784), a former pupil and foreman of Brown.[4]

North Cray's landscape still reflects its late-18th century 'Arcadian' landscape with its ribbon-like lake, reduced in width from its 18th-century appearance but still spanned by its key crossing point - an elegant and aptly-named Five Arch Bridge. Built largely of brick, it bears similarities to other bridges by or attributed to Brown such as at Temple Newsham, Charlcote and Compton Verney. These, however, are more refined and built in stone which may suggest either that Brown or his client preferred the use of vernacular materials or that cost was a factor. The writer and essayist, Charles Lamb (1775-1834), who as a child had known Coventry, wrote:

> Thomas Coventry passed his youth in contracted
> circumstances, which gave him early those
> parsimonious habits which in after life never forsook
> him; so that, with one windfall or another, about the
> time I knew him he was master of four or five hundred
> thousand pounds ... a hoarder rather than a miser ...
> Coventry gave away £30,000 at once in his life time to a
> blind charity.'[5]

The Five Arch Bridge incorporates a weir and downstream are the remains of a brickwork sluice. The parkland contains a scatter of mature deciduous trees and some isolated, mature, and probably 18th-century Cedar of Lebanon survive within

housing near the site of the former North Cray house. A narrow
wooded strip either side of the River Cray which formed part
of 19th-century walks now consists of mainly 20th-century
deciduous trees. Much of the once-open parkland along the
river's banks is fragmented into small grassy spaces and its
tree-framed vistas are lost to 20th-century scrub and secondary
woodland, particularly those views westwards to the parkland
of Foots Cray Place and to the river itself, except where it
widens upstream from the bridge. A large section of the park to
the south has been lost to 20th-century housing and its north-
east corner to allotments. One or two isolated features survive
from the early 18th-century layout including the principal
section of a drive which crosses the bridge westwards to a
former lodge in the north-west corner of the estate, in North
Cray Wood. The eastern half of this wood probably survives
due to its designation as ancient woodland. A single lodge (one
of a pair) also survives beside the former main approach to the
estate from the south-east, off the North Cray Road, as do the
walls of the kitchen garden and a bothy (shelter for the head
gardener).

Although so little survives of North Cray's landscape before its
late-18th century transformation, there is sufficient evidence
from documents, maps and illustrations to present at least a
partial picture of its extent and appearance before Coventry
commissioned Brown. The estate had changed hands several
times, including through several generations of the Bowes
family, between the 12th century and its purchase in c.1738
by Jeffrey Hetherington, whose family is commemorated by a
surviving and imposing gateway with ornate gates in the south-
west wall of St James' churchyard which once led directly into
the park. The earliest record of a house, south of St James'
church, dates from the early 17th century, presumably built by
the Bowes family and this seems to have survived until it was
rebuilt in the 1820s.[6]

The Andrews, Dury and Herbert map of 1769 is the earliest
record of any designed gardens around North Cray Place. It
shows a formal landscape comprising pleasure grounds laid
out with paths and water features appearing to extend north-
west from the house across the River Cray as far as North

Cray Wood. Various buildings are scattered around, perhaps providing for outdoor pursuits such as fishing, boating or taking refreshment, some concentrated at the river's edge at the point where a drive or path crosses the river towards North Cray Wood, and on the site of the Five Arch Bridge (fig.1).

An engraving by Bayly (fig.2), some 10 years later and just a year after Coventry inherited, shows an imposing three-storey building with one tower at each corner, formal geometric terraced gardens including a variety of shrubs, specimen trees and areas laid to lawn. The gardens to the south-east of the house are divided into rectangular areas by rows of planting, and avenues of trees lead north-west to the river. The church of St James, about 250 metres south-east of the river at the point where the Five Arch Bridge was later to be built, is connected directly to the house through a gateway in its south-west wall. From the house, Coventry would have had a clear view of Foots Cray Place which had already begun its transformation to a more naturalistic appearance as depicted in an engraving by Woollett of c.1760 (fig.3).

While Woollett's print shows elements of an earlier, more formal style, the wider landscape shows the influence of early exponents of more naturalistic landscaping styles, such as

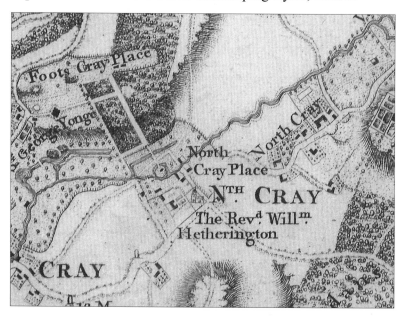

**Figure 1.
Andrews, Dury and
Herbert map, 1769**
*Courtesy: Kent
History and Library
Centre*

94

Figure 2. (above)
Engraving of North
Cray Place by J.
Bayly c.1779 looking
north-west
*Courtesy: Bexley
Local Studies and
Archive Centre*
Figure 3. (below)
Engraving of Foots
Cray Place c.1760
by William Woollett,
looking east towards
North Cray estate
*Courtesy: Bexley
Local Studies and
Archive Centre*

Bridgeman and Kent, which Brown would later develop to their
full potential.

Foots Cray's new Palladian villa, built in 1754 for Bouchier
Cleve, was situated on a rise and its predominantly open,
grassed landscape extended right up to the house.[7] A narrow,
canal-like expanse of water running north-south across the
estate is crossed by an elegant single-arched bridge leading into
sparsely-planted parkland with its herd of deer in the middle
distance. The Andrews, Dury and Herbert map of 1769 (fig.1)
confirms how the openness of this landscape takes advantage
of the long distance views across the canal towards North Cray
Place, the buildings of which may, in Woollett's print, just be
seen, again on a slight promontory and backed by trees.

Although based on a map dating from a little later (1810),
Oliver Wooller in his book The Great Estates describes the
scene depicted by Woollett:

'the River Cray was dammed to create a meandering reservoir (later referred to as a canal) lying between the church (All Saints, Foots Cray) shrouded behind a cherry orchard at the southern end of the park ...To the north the new house overlooked the lake (reservoir/ canal) across a wide lawn from its promontory above the western shore. The waters of the stream were diverted by a canal to the east from which a cascade flowed down to the lake (canal) in full view of the house ... Walks and bridle paths were laid out across the park and a bridge flung over the river... '.[9]

The scene is first accurately surveyed on the Ordnance Survey drawing of 1799.

During the 18th century, North Cray and Foots Cray and other nearby districts such as Bexley and Bexleyheath, within relatively easy reach of London and Westminster, were popular country retreats for wealthy City merchants, aldermen, politicians and former Lord Mayors of London. Between 1710 and 1740, some two thirds of the grand houses built were owned by Members of Parliament, many of these land holdings created from the land of older and larger estates. Land ownership demonstrated status and could be effective in successfully commanding rural votes; a grand house, built in the latest fashion and surrounded by gardens, water and parkland represented prestige and authority. Land also now provided better income from much improved methods of agriculture.[9]

Contemporary with Foots Cray, both nearby Danson (9 kilometres north-west at Bexleyheath) and Vale Mascal (3 kilometres north of North Cray Place and built on land forming part of the Mount Mascal estate),[10] underwent improvements from 1760 to 1773 and 1760 to 1775 respectively, both of which Coventry would have seen on his arrival as illustrating something that he might achieve for his own estate. Estate owners were heavily influenced by each other's aspirations for the latest style and were frequently connected through business or marriage; for example, the small villa at Vale Mascal in 1746 was built for Thomas Tash (son of Sir John Tash, alderman and former Lord Mayor of London) who had married the cousin

Figure 5.
Danson Hill, engraved by James Heath from a
drawing by Richard Corbould, 1794 illustrating the
lake below the parkland and mansion
Courtesy: Bexley Local Studies and Archive Centre

Figure 4.
The River Cray at Vale Mascal with rustic bridge
and weir c.1890
Courtesy: Bexley Local Studies and Archive Centre

of two wealthy local men from the nearby estates of Mayplace
and Hall Place. Danson's tenant in 1753 was Sir John Boyd,
the wealthy son of a West Indian sugar planter and director of
the East India Company. He had connections with Sir Henry
Vansittart, also a director of the East India Company whose
son Sir Nicholas Vansittart, (knighted as Lord Bexley in 1823)
became owner of Foots Cray Place on his father's death in
c.1767.

Both Danson and Vale Mascal (fig.4) and, beyond, Loring Hall
(sometimes known as Woollett Hall and dating from c.1760),
show clear similarities with Brown's work and with that of
Richmond who was probably working at Danson from about
1760 until about 1773 although attribution is still uncertain.
Either Richmond or possibly Richard Woods (1715/16-1793),
one of the most well-known imitators of Brown's style who
lived and worked on similar estates in Essex, was working
at Vale Mascal between 1760 and 1775. Fiona Cowell in
her biography of Woods describes how a number of Brown's
contemporaries often worked on the same estates: *'Brown took
over from Woods at New Wardour Castle and Woods followed
Brown at Chillington and Audley End.'* [11]

Figure 6.
Chapel House c.1900, an eye catcher on the boundary of the Danson estate
Courtesy: Bexley Local Studies and Archive Centre
Figure 7.
Andrews, Dury and Herbert map of Danson Hill estate, 1769
Courtesy: Kent History and Library Centre

In 1762, Sir John Boyd had become the absolute owner of Danson[12] and soon made his mark with a new Palladian-style mansion (fig.5) designed by Sir Robert Taylor and with internal fittings by Sir William Chambers.[13] Completed by 1768, Danson overlooks the valley of the Danson stream with its two ponds or 'Basons' and ornamental canal. Both Taylor and Chambers frequently worked closely with Brown on similar sized estates and Brown was working with Chambers at Ingress at the time the Danson mansion was completed. Various other buildings decorated the landscape including a Doric Temple and a cottage transformed into a folly, renamed Chapel house (fig.6), with a spire and Gothic-style windows, to act as an eye-catcher on the skyline in the view from the main house.[14]

This transformation of domestic buildings into ornamental, often Gothicised, picturesque landscape features was very much in Brown's oeuvre; another example is the conversion of a 17th-century pigeon house into a chapel at Leeds Abbey. Boyd then turned his attention to the landscape and demolished the old house and its outbuildings (fig.7).

Drawing on Ruth Hutcherson's book History of Danson, Wooller describes the major changes undertaken and attributed to Richmond: *'In 1773 the Danson stream was dammed, flooding the site of the old house to create a deep lake'*. He goes on to describe the landscape:

> *'Across this expanse of water lay the woods of Bexley*
> *Park to the south. A river like extension of the lake*
> *twined around the house to the west beyond rose the*

98

heights of Shooters Hill, while to the east a curtain of trees hid the outbuildings, kitchen gardens and ice well. To the north, beyond the driveway the fortunate residents could view a magnificent panorama of rolling countryside culminating in the Thames...For those who cared to walk or ride, Richmond mapped out a gravel path, which crossed *the lake and skirted the boundaries of the park. ....'.*[15]

Richmond had previously worked for Brown for five years at Moor Park, Rickmansworth (1754-59) and would have gained extensive knowledge and experience from remodelling the pleasure grounds, earth-moving and creating a serpentine lake. The landscape at Danson is still recognisable today with its serpentine lake and parkland. Vale Mascal's landscape, however, is much reduced, with the original house and most of its grounds having been separated from the remainder in 1935.

At Vale Mascal, the River Cray followed a course of meanders and channels through the estate with formal pathways crossing various bridges to islands, a pond, and a series of weirs, a cascade and a waterwheel (fig.8). The first written account by Hasted in 1797 refers to 'the beautiful cascade'.[16] However, its most notable feature is the bath house (fig.9), built in 1766

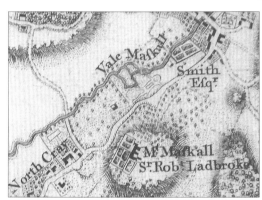

Figure 8.
Andrews, Dury and Herbert map of Vale Mascal estate, 1769
Courtesy: Kent History and Library Centre
Figure 9.
Vale Mascal Bath House c.1910
Courtesy: Bexley Local Studies and Archive Centre

and likely to have been designed by Woods, who is best known for the design of intimate pleasure grounds and gardens.[17] As an amateur architect, he also designed garden structures; his rustic 'cold bath' incorporating a cascade at New Wardour Castle, Wiltshire is contemporary with Vale Mascal's bath house. Such bath houses were fashionable and that at Vale Mascal was an unusual feature, displaying the type of hydraulic ingenuity often associated with Brown's skill and inventiveness in managing water.

The building itself is in the Gothic style, designed to look like a small chapel complete with sham tower, buttressed walls and Gothic windows. It housed a cold plunge pool and was situated on one of the channels which flowed around a number of islands. Given that the River Cray has a very gradual gradient here, it would have required significant hydraulic inventiveness to achieve satisfactory water inflow and discharge. The bath house was fed via a sluice gate on an almost level channel about 150 feet downstream from a weir. A further internal sluice gate operated on the outfall pipe of the bath which discharged down a slight slope back into the Cray. This enabled the bath to be filled to a level of 4 feet and completely drained when required.

Although the landscape features on these estates all required skill in managing and engineering water, it was Brown who really brought its imaginative and practical use to perfection. He often created vast lakes, built complex cascades and weirs to control flow, disguised changes in level to allow vistas to flow unimpeded across the landscape and, as one practical device, allowed silt to be deposited to ensure increased oxygen to water to improve fish stocks.[18] At both North Cray and Vale Mascal the creation of islands and inlets may have served as duck decoys for both fishing and shooting.

Thomas Coventry inherited North Cray in 1778 from the Reverend William Hetherington, a relative, probably a cousin. Coventry would therefore almost certainly have known the house and landscape, and been a guest at neighbouring new houses and newly-landscaped estates through his social standing as Treasurer at the Temple, a sub-governor of the

South Sea Company and as a Member of Parliament. He was born into an already long-established aristocratic family which had held their seat at Croome in Worcestershire continuously from about 1600. His uncle was William, the 5th Earl of Coventry (1678-1751) and his cousin, George, was the 6th Earl – *'The Grave Young Lord of the remains of the Patriot Breed.'[19]* The younger brother of the 5th Earl, his father, Thomas Coventry senior, was a Russian merchant married to Mary Green; Thomas junior was their second son. In c.1743, he married Margaret Savage, a distant relation through marriage. Margaret's mother's first marriage had been to the 5th Baron and 1st Earl, Thomas Coventry, and she had inherited his huge personal estate. Coventry junior became a wealthy man being a successful lawyer at Sergeants Inn Fleet Street, London and MP for Bridport from 1754 to 1780 following other members of the Coventry family who had held that seat yearly since 1708.[20]

Very soon after inheriting, Coventry instructed Brown to carry out alterations to the estate. Brown's account book records that in 1781-82 he was paid a total of £1,300 by Coventry for work at North Cray.[21] This was a substantial sum, the equivalent of at least £150,000 today, and when compared with payments to Brown for commissions for similar estates would certainly have been sufficient for the scale and style of alterations which Coventry required.

**Figure 10.
North Cray Place c.1933 showing mature trees in the pleasure grounds around the house and grazed meadows adjacent to the river**
Courtesy: Bexley Local Studies and Archive Centre

The alterations comprised the smoothing and widening of a section of the meandering River Cray to form a ribbon-like lake controlled by a weir and sluices, the stopping up of an inconvenient footpath within view of the house[22], earthmoving and probably drainage of the water meadows, the creation of parkland with clumps and enclosing boundary tree belts and a series of walks and drives around the estate (fig.10). It has been suggested in a research report carried out for English Heritage in 2013 that these tree belts may have been inspired by the narrow linear woods found in areas subject to old-enclosure and known as 'shaws' in Kent. However, what is certainly likely is that Brown approached his commission holistically by 'borrowing' Foots Cray's already semi-naturalistic landscape of water and open parkland to create one whole compositional piece.

Croome had been Brown's first serious independent commission and one which occupied him for several decades from 1747 to 1782, during which time he developed a close relationship with the Earl. Thomas Coventry presumably would have had every opportunity to observe - and later to emulate - the revolutionary transformation of Croome's marshy, infertile and low value agricultural land into an ordered, agriculturally-productive but aesthetically pleasing parkland. Brown had also demonstrated his skills as an architect, his first major design being the Palladian-style house at Croome Court (1751-52) later followed by the re-location of St Mary of Magdalene church as an 'eye catcher'.[23]

Brown's fee of £5000 indicates the size and extent of the Croome commission; Thomas Coventry, a cousin of William Coventry the 6th Earl, would probably have been suitably impressed by the scale and impact on the landscape that could be obtained from vast earth and drainage works. At Croome:

> 'The river was extended to trace a meandering course and its upper end now curved west to meet the new lake. It reflects the curving course of the River Severn a mile or so to the west as a complement to this important natural feature of the local landscape'.[24]

The parkland was ornamented with large clumps and belts of trees traversed by circuit drives and walks (a three mile walk and a ten mile drive) so that the landscaping could be admired at close quarters. By the early 1780s, the third phase of drainage was underway and the early planting was maturing.[25] All this could well have influenced Thomas Coventry's ideas for both the design and practical management of his estate.

The location of the main house at both North Cray and Foots Cray, on elevated ground above the river, suggests a desire to avoid the low-lying water meadows and consequently giving them good views while enjoying dry ground close to the house. The River Cray is a chalk river with some wide, shallow gravel sections so, to create a lake, Brown would have used both his skill and experience in manipulating water, using either a mixture of wet clay and sand or puddling clay to create a watertight lining on porous soils, such as he almost certainly did at Valence lining the Middle Lake with clay in the early 1770s. It may be that abstraction for the reservoir or canal at Foots Cray and the water features at Vale Mascal had lowered the river's water level at North Cray, forcing Brown to design his lake with a central 'neck' incorporating a bridge, weir and two islands; this was aesthetically pleasing but also had the practical purpose of keeping the lake filled. There had been a corn mill at Foots Cray since the 16th century and by 1742 a paper mill took over the same site and continued until the 1900s. Since paper-making requires substantial amounts of water, it may be the case that abstraction for this purpose changed the nature of the river so that it ran dry in periods of low rainfall. Low water levels may have remained a problem into the 20th century as the Ordnance Survey 3rd edition (1905-1910) shows several new features upstream from the bridge including a hydraulic ram at Foots Cray Place. At the beginning of his career, as described by Steffie Shields, Brown had gained both skill and experience in hydraulics by working on fen navigation schemes in Lincolnshire,[26] and soon after:

> *'The 1740's saw several years of devastating drought. Brown spent ten years at Stowe...besides addressing water issues for neighbouring landowners. The following decade saw unprecedented rainfall and an increased demand for his services ....Clients, facing several years of disruption, were persuaded that serious*

investment in hydraulic schemes and plantations would bring huge benefits from grazing and forestry.'[27]

Shields continues by describing how Lincolnshire's agricultural improvers influenced Brown's methods. They had used the managed flooding of water meadows ('floating' irrigation) and, by maintaining a constant flow of water, fields were fertilised thus reducing the effects of frost and gaining an early growth of grass and a further hay crop later on.

The Tithe map of 1838 (fig.11) and the 1st Edition Ordnance Survey Map, 1858-73 (fig.12) record Brown's planting approaching maturity. Although Coventry himself did not survive long enough to see the new mixed planting of deciduous and coniferous species reach this stage, he must have taken pleasure in the serpentine lake with its islands, the elegant bridge, the entrance drives and the estates walks and rides all eminently fitting for his business and social standing. There are various belts and clumps of both deciduous and coniferous trees strategically placed to control views; for example, the main approach drive enters through a boundary tree belt, continues across open grazing land between two clumps about half way

Figure 11.
Tithe map, 1838
Courtesy: Kent History and Library Centre

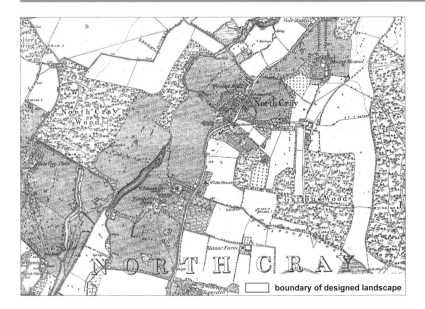

Figure 12.
1st Edition Ordnance Survey map, 1858-73, showing boundary of designed landscape in early 1780s
Courtesy: Bexley Local Studies and Archive Centre

to the house, which is hidden by a tree belt until within a short distance of the frontage. A clear example of a typical Brown feature is a circuit walk from the house which leads south-west through a belt of trees and towards the farm buildings; it crosses a small stream, then the river at the lake's southern end to head north-west to North Cray Wood, from where it returns to complete its route across parkland to the Five Arch Bridge and back to the house. The small stream may be there to assist drainage but contributes to the scenery as a feature in its own right. One unusual planting feature is an open area, oval in shape and edged with trees, to the north of the house. However, the boundary tree belts, which are such a typical Brown feature, are clearly seen fully screening the road and North Cray village on the north-east boundary and south-east boundaries. There is a very carefully angled view due north between two oval clumps towards the lake and the view west from the house across the parkland and lake culminates with a tree belt, thus screening the house of Foots Cray Place whilst 'borrowing' its landscape. A belt of planting to the south, and a brick boundary wall against the road to the east, screen the ornamental gardens directly east of the house. The church itself is also screened by planting to the north, south and south-west and to the east, where the kitchen gardens are enclosed by brick boundary walls.

Very few changes occur to the tree pattern and landscape features over the next hundred or so years, except for the removal of the two clumps about halfway along the main approach drive and one of the oval clumps, formerly planted north-west of the house. An additional path or drive across the parkland is shown, leading directly to the farm buildings south-west of the house towards the river. The 17th-century house has been demolished and rebuilt in 1822-23 in the 'Adam' style of Portland stone and black marble. By 1910, the 3rd edition Ordnance Survey map of 1905-10 shows that an additional water or drainage feature has appeared, comprising a large pond on the south-eastern edge of North Cray Wood, which flows into a stream crossing the parkland, incorporates a weir, and ends in a small pond.

Until his death in c.1850, Lord Bexley, who lived at Foots Cray Place, leased much of the estate including North Cray Place itself to a series of tenants. Between 1905 and 1930, both estates were owned by Robert Arnold Vansittart, and in 1908 the house, and presumably some of the grounds, were let to North Kent Golf Club Ltd making use of the Brown landscape for various sporting activities including golf, croquet, archery, lawn tennis, bowls, fishing and boating (fig. 13). By 1910, the property had been sold again and by 1931 it was advertised for sale as valuable building land, illustrating that the changes in the social makeup and economics of the area were beginning to take place. Initially, part of the south-east corner was developed with houses and bungalows with further housing built in 1965 on the site of the house. Since being owned by the local authority, the estates of both North Cray and Foots Cray have been maintained as an informal open space;

Figure 13.
North Cray Place
grounds in use as a
golf course looking
north- west c.1910
Courtesy: Bexley Local
Studies and Archive
Centre

and, here, Brown's Five Arch Bridge has been maintained to a degree, although much of it has been rebuilt: the original red brick has largely been replaced with yellow brick, except at each end, and the stone parapet is now mainly render (fig.14). The main drive from the church across the bridge towards North Cray Wood is still in situ but now surfaced with tarmac. The lines of other paths have been lost and replaced with new ones of worn grass made by visitors' desire lines. The southern part of the lake now contains a series of mid-to-late 20th century islands, and the lake and river appear to be well maintained. While the parkland has lost its 18th-century tree groupings and belts, several coniferous specimens, including cedars, were planted in the 20th century within the area formerly to the south-west of the house. A few mature Cedars of Lebanon and the 19th-century red-brick walls to the kitchen garden survive, incorporated into housing. Much of the original North Cray landscape is a local nature reserve and an oasis of semi-natural habitats within a suburban setting; the marshy land adjacent to the River Cray in particular is diverse with several uncommon plants. 'The Alders' wet woodland and North Cray Wood are also important for wildlife. The river itself is possibly London's best for water quality, with

**Figure 14.
North Cray Place
looking south-west
showing the lake,
bridge and parkland
2015**
*Courtesy: Lee Ricketts
taken from youtu.be/
rGMJd3ml37Y*

107

a relatively naturally-graded profile, and its course can be followed from the Meadows along a 16 kilometre footpath to its confluence with the River Thames at Erith, passing Vale Mascal and Hall Place en-route.

Wooller concludes:
> *'We can see in the past century, suburbia transformed Bexley from a cluster of country villages lying beside the seats of great lords and lesser squires into a borough of the once distant City of London, a further inundation of the land, by the new, new, new nobility – the middle class commuter'.*[28]

Today, little remains as a reminder of the prominence of estates such as Foots Cray and North Cray Place, and most of the other grand houses within Bexley Borough have also gone. Danson,

Loring Hall and Hall Place have survived with the house and grounds of both Danson and Hall Place now in public ownership.[29] Foots Cray Place was destroyed by fire in 1949, and demolished in 1950; and North Cray Place was demolished in 1962. However, the attractions of the River Cray and specifically the essential components of Brown's work, the lake and the Five Arch Bridge (fig.15) are largely unchanged and the parkland remains, although its size and mature tree cover are much reduced. The public open space (fig.14) of Foots Cray Meadows is an example of how the constituents of an 18th-century landscape - parkland, mature trees and water features - are timeless in their attractiveness, and particularly those designed by Brown, which, as Shields describes, outclass all others in artistic eye for line, scale and variety.[30] They perhaps also exemplify a common vision of the traditional 'English Landscape' made so fashionable by Brown and his followers.

**Figure 15.
The Lake and Five
Arch Bridge looking
north 2015**
*Courtesy: Lee Ricketts
taken from youtu.be/
rGMJd3ml37Y*

References

1   Hasted (1972 edition), vol.2, p.135

2   Wooller, p.47 Nicholas Vansittart (Lord Bexley) was the son of Henry Vansittart, a Director of the East India Company himself connected to John Boyd, also a Director of the East India Company and the owner of Danson.

3   Ibid. p.52 At the end of the Second World War, Foots Cray Place and its grounds were bought by Kent County Council with the intention of converting them into a museum and park. Later, in the late 1950s, both Foots Cray Place and North Cray Place and their grounds were acquired by Sidcup and Chislehurst Urban District Councils.

4   Ibid. pp.63-64 The attribution of Danson is unclear, but Wooller refers to Richmond's map dated 1770 and David Jacques' Georgian Gardens: The Reign of Nature (1983); also the Parks & Gardens UK website attributes to Richmond a plan dated 1762-3. A historical survey by Colson Stone (1997) confirms that some elements of Richmond's plan were implemented. R. Hutcherson A History of Danson pp.18-20 states that John Boyd's 'head' gardener, Fean Garwood, came from one of the estates Brown worked on and may have heard a conversation between Brown and Richmond about the location of a new dam to create the lake.

5   www.historyofparliamentonline.org The History of Parliament: the House of Commons 1754 -1790 (ed. Sir Lewis Namier)

6   Gammons, p.23 St James' church was the private chapel of the Bowes family.

7   Wooller, p.42 The original house at Foots Cray was Pike Place built in c.1566 and passed to Bouchier Cleve in 1752 (Bexley Local Studies and Archives Centre U855/T1/1/19)

8   Ibid. pp.44-45

9   Ibid. p.45

10   Vale Mascal was built on part of the Mount Mascal estate whose main house, Mascals Mount, having been rebuilt in the early 1600s, may have been intended to serve as the Dower House.

11   Cowell, preface, xix

12   Wooller, p.61 John Boyd was a tenant for 21 years before acquiring two quarter shares of the estate in 1759 and further shares in 1762.

13   Hutcherson, p.13 Sir Robert Taylor, the architect of Danson Hill, admired Italian Palladian villas and knew the copies made by English architects, including Foots Cray Place; however, Danson Hill was a weekend retreat and his design was for an elegant family home in the country not too far from London and the City, where Boyd would have also had a town house. It was completed by 1770.

14   Ibid. p.18 The architect of Chapel House is unknown but it is first shown with its spire on the Andrews, Dury and Herbert map of 1769 together with the new house Danson Hill; however, the grounds still comprise the original two ponds, an ornamental canal, and the old Danson House and its outbuildings remain. See also pp.15 & 36: the designer of the Doric Temple, Sir William Chambers, designed ceilings, chimney pieces and cornices for Danson Hill and also a Palladian bridge. The temple was commissioned in 1770, dismantled in 1961, restored and moved to St Paul's Walden Bury, Hertfordshire.

15   Wooller, pp.63-64

16   Hasted (1972 edition), vol.2, pp.141- 2

17   Hickman. The author describes Wood's rustic design for the cold bath at New Wardour Castle, grounds by Brown.

110

18   Shields, p.39
19   Gordon, p.86 refers to the 6th Earl's ambitions, with Horace Walpole generous enough
        to describe him as the 'grave young Lord'.
20   www.historyofparliamentonline.org op.cit.
21   Royal Horticultural Society Lindley Libraries, The Account Book of Lancelot Brown,
        1764-1788 (unpublished manuscript), p.149 Thomas Coventry Esq. North Cray: 1781
        September 9th Rec'd £500, 1782 January 11th Rec'd £300, May 23rd. Rec'd £200,
        September 17th.Rec'd £300. All were settled by the executors in 1782.
22   Kent History & Library Centre, footpath change in 1782, Q/RH/2/12
23   Gordon, p.105, and pp.118-119 Much of the work at Croome was carried out between
        Brown and the architect, Robert Adam, including the church which was started by
        Brown and completed by Adam in 1761; from the porch and tower there were
        panoramic views across the park illustrating the extent of Brown's talent.
24   Ibid. p.116 The initial stage of the landscaping was designed by Brown.
25   Gordon, p.124
26   Shields, p.38
27   Ibid.
28   Wooller, p.107
29   Ibid. pp. 5 and 20 The original manor, including the site of the present house, Hall
        Place, built sometime between 1537 and 1540, is recorded in the Domesday Book. In
        1935, the trustees of the son-in-law of the tenant May, Countess of Limerick, sold the
        house and twenty five acres to Bexley Council, subject to a life tenancy for the
        Countess.
30   Shields, p.39

Bibliography

Bellamy, G.A. *An Apology for the Life of George Anne Bellamy* (London, 1785)

Beltramini, G. and Burns, H. (eds.) *Palladio* (Royal Academy of Arts, London, 2008)

Brayley, E.W. *The Beauties of England and Wales* (London, 1808)

Brown, J. *The Omnipotent Magician: Lancelot 'Capability' Brown, 1716-1783* (Chatto and Windus, London, 2011)

Burke, J. (ed.) *A Genealogical and Heraldic History of the Landed Gentry* (London, 1838)

Caiger, J.E.L. *Two Pigeon Houses* (Archaeologia Cantiana, 1974)

Capon, L. *Early Roman Features, Possibly Defensive, and the Modern Development of the Parkland and Landscape at Ingress Abbey, Greenhithe* (Archaeologia Cantiana, 2009)

Chambers, W. *Designs of Chinese Buildings, Furniture, Dresses, Machines and Utensils* (London, 1757)

Chambers, W. *A Dissertation on Oriental Gardening* (London, 1772)

Courtney, W.P. and Woodland Rev P. *Oxford Dictionary of National Biography: Calcraft, John, the elder (bap.1726-1772)* (Oxford University Press, 2004-2015)

Cowell, F. *Richard Woods (1715-1793): Master of the Pleasure Garden* (The Boydell Press, Woodbridge, 2009)

Dugdale, W. *Monasticon Anglicanum* (London, 1849)

Fielding, C.H. *Leeds Priory* (Invicta Magazine, volume II, no.4, 1912)

Finnegan, R.J. *The Classical Taste of William Ponsonby, 2nd Earl of Bessborough* (Irish Architectural and Decorative Studies: The Journal of the Georgian Society, 2005)

Fisher, T. *The History and Antiquities of Rochester* (Rochester, 1772)

Fisher, T. *The Kentish Traveller's Companion* (London, 1776)

Gammons, J. *A History of North Cray* (North Cray Residents' Association, 2012)

Gordon, C. *The Coventrys Of Croome* (Trustees of the Croome Estate, 2000)

Gilpin, W. *A Journey through Kent* (London, 1774)

Grant, F. *Glasshouses* (Shire Publications, Oxford, 2013)

Harris, J. *History of Kent* (London, 1719)

Harris, J. (et al) *Sir William Chambers* (Zwemmer, London, 1970)

Harris, J. *Sir William Chambers, Architect to George III* (Yale University and the Courtauld Institute of Art, 1996)

Hasted, E. *The History and Topographical Survey of the County of Kent* (first edition, Canterbury, 1790)

Hasted, E. *The History and Topographical Survey of the County of Kent* (W. Bristow, Canterbury, 1797-1801, republished: EP Publishing, Wakefield, Yorkshire, 1972)

Hickman, C. *Taking the Plunge, C18 bath houses and plunge pools* (www.buildingconservation.com, 2010)

Hutcherson, R. *History of Danson* (Bexley Leisure Services Department, 1996)

Jenkins, S. *England's Thousand Best Houses* (Penguin Books, England, 2003)

Jennings, A. *Georgian Gardens* (English Heritage, 2005)

Jessup, R.F. FSA *Thomas Heron of Chilham* (Archaeologia Cantiana, 1943)

Lennon, B. *A study of the trees of Savernake Forest and Tottenham Park, Wiltshire, using statistical analysis of stem diameter* (Garden History, Journal of the Garden History Society, Winter 2014, The Lavenham Press Ltd, 2014)

Lochen, J.R. *Valence: a Changing Landscape: A History of the Estate and its People* (published privately, 1992)

Marshall, P. *Oxford Dictionary of National Biography: Hills, Wills (1718-1793), first Marquess of Downshire, politician* (Oxford University Press, 2004-2015)

Mason, W. *An Heroic Epistle in Answer to Sir William Chambers, Knight* (London, 1773)

Mayer, L. *Capability Brown and the English Landscape Garden* (Shire Publications, Oxford, 2011)

Neale, J.P. *Views of the Seats of Noblemen and Gentlemen in England, Wales, Scotland and Ireland* (1819)

Phibbs, J. *A list of landscapes that have been attributed to Lancelot Capability Brown* (Garden History, Journal of the Garden History Society, Winter 2013, The Lavenham Press Ltd, 2013)

Philipott, T. *Villare Cantianum of Kent, Surveyed and Illustrated* (1659)

Pococke, R. *Travels through England* (1888 edition)

Remington, V. *Painting Paradise - the Art of the Garden* (Royal Collection Trust, 2015)

Seymour, C. *A New Topographical, Historical, and Commercial Survey of the Cities, Towns, and Villages of the County of Kent* (Canterbury, 1776)

Shields, S. *Golden moments of landscape* (Lincolnshire Life, May 2015)

Stone, M. (et al) *An eighteenth-century obsession – the plant collection of the 6th earl of Coventry at Croome Park, Worcestershire* (Garden History, Journal of the Garden History Society, Summer 2015, The Lavenham Press Ltd, 2015)

Stroud, D. *Henry Holland, His Life and Architecture* (Country Life, 1966)

Stroud, D. *Capability Brown* (Faber and Faber, first edition 1950, second edition 1975)

Taylor, W.S and Pringle, J.H. (eds.) *Correspondence of William Pitt, Earl of Chatham* (London, 1840)

Tester, P.J. *Leeds Priory; the Claustral Buildings* (Archaeologia Cantiana, 1979)

Vuillamy, L. *List of Works Completed* (Builder XXIX, 1871)

Watkin, D. *English Architecture - a concise history* (Thames and Hudson, London, 1979)

Watts, W. *Seats of the Nobility and Gentry* (John & Josiah Boydell, 1779)

White, R. *Oxford Dictionary of National Biography: Vardy, John (1717/18- 1765)* (Oxford University Press, 2004-2015)

Williamson, T. *Polite Landscapes – Gardens and Society in Eighteenth-Century England* (Sutton Publishing, 1995)

Willis, P. *Capability Brown's Account with Drummonds Bank* (Architectural History, volume 27, 1984)

Wooller, O. *The Great Estates* (Bexley Local Studies and Archive Centre, 2000)